YOU'VE GOT PICTURES!
AOL'S GUIDE TO DIGITAL IMAGING

YOU'VE GOT PICTURES! AOL'S GUIDE TO DIGITAL IMAGING

Edited by Seth Godin

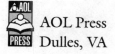

AOL Press
Dulles, VA

You've Got Pictures! AOL's Guide to Digital Imaging

The figures in this book were created for the sole purpose of demonstrating the capabilities of digital imaging software. Some contain fictitious content and may include photographs posted on the AOL service by its members. No figure in the book may be reproduced or altered in any manner.

Editorial Director: Brad Schepp
Interior and Cover Design: Karen Engelmann

© 1998 by America Online, Inc.

America Online is a registered service mark of America Online, Inc.

Printed in the United States of America

98 99 00 10 9 8 7 6 5 4 3

Library of Congress Cataloging-in-Publication Data
Godin, Seth.
　　You've Got Pictures! AOL's Guide to Digital Imaging/by Seth Godin.
　　　　p.　　　cm.
　　Includes index.
　　Library of Congress Catalog Card Number: 98-71566
　　ISBN: 1-891556-51-7

GREETINGS FROM AMERICA ONLINE!

Welcome to AOL Press, creator of official, authoritative guides straight from America Online. Each book is written just for you, our members.

With so many books published every year, especially about online stuff, you may be wondering what makes an AOL Press book different.

Glad you asked.

We develop and write AOL Press books with our members' needs in mind—always. To develop these books, we consulted with you at every step. First, we asked you just which topics you'd like to see AOL cover. We then made sure we included the information you wanted, in a friendly way. That means jargon-free and emphasizing the practical.

We also remembered that you're online not only to get things done, but also to have some fun along the way.

This book will open a new world to you—the world of computer pictures. You'll learn how it's now as easy to send pictures online as it is to send words. We hope you have as much fun exploring this book, as we did creating it.

See you online,

Brad Schepp
Editorial Director
America Online

ACKNOWLEDGMENTS

With special thanks to Elisabeth Parker for her essential contributions, and to Kathryn Toyer for her help.

At Seth Godin Productions, thanks to Nana Sledzieski, Wendy Wax, Lisa DiMona, Linda Carbone, Lisa Lindsay, Perri Knize, Shelley Flannery, Rachel Thompson, Susan Kushnick, and Katherine Kendall.

At AOL, thanks to Brad Schepp, John Tierney, Judy Karpinski, John Dyn, Don Crowl, and Paul DiVito.

CONTENTS

ix

YOU'VE GOT PICTURES!
AOL'S GUIDE TO DIGITAL IMAGING

INTRODUCTION

Look around you. Chances are you've filled your home or workspace with pictures: a collection of family photos, a snapshot from a blissful Paris honeymoon, three paintings by your four-year-old, a funny cartoon you clipped from the paper.

Pictures are worth more than a thousand words. They evoke memories that touch our hearts. They start conversations. They win (or lose) political campaigns. But not unless they're shared.

This book is about sharing pictures. Remember when desktop publishing made it possible for anyone to create book- or magazine-style pages? Or when e-mail sparked an instantaneous communications revolution? A third revolution is upon us. Now, with America Online and the Web, anyone can publish any image. You can share pictures from that three-day canoe trip with your college buddies, or let people see electron microscope images you created at work.

Suddenly, you can use images online to persuade, to cajole, to make people laugh or cry. You can gather your extended family in a chat room and reminisce about the old days, or create funny holiday cards and save on postage. It's all possible with digital imaging. Simply put, that means "putting pictures on a computer." And it's really easy.

Try it right now. Go to keyword **Gallery** to get to the AOL Portrait Gallery on the AOL service and click on Tour the Galleries.

1. In the listbox that appears, doubleclick on Portrait Gallery Highlights Image Library. (It's got a little software icon next to it, which means you can download pictures here.)

2. Take your pick of pictures. We liked Amelia Earhart, the American aviator. Highlight the name and click on Download Now.

3. Save the file to your America Online downloads directory.

You just put a digital image on your computer. See? We told you it wasn't hard.

It's easy to get *your own* pictures on your computer too. You don't even need to buy any special equipment. All you have to do is take a roll of film (or a bunch of negatives) to the photo lab and have them make a floppy image disk or a photo CD for you. Many photo labs offer this service for about the same cost as having a regular roll of film developed.

What You'll Learn

After reading a few chapters of this book, you'll be able to:

1. Turn your vacation photos into a CD and e-mail them to your traveling companions in Mexico.

2. Include the travel photos in a Web site that you build on AOL.

3. Scan in your child's artwork and use it to create a birthday invitation that you can e-mail to his friends.

4. Take your photo with a digital camera and post it in the singles section online in the hope of finding a dream date.

5. Research old photos online and find a long-lost relative. Download her picture and add it to your family's scrapbook.

As a bonus, you'll be capable of putting Winston Churchill's head on Teri Hatcher's body. Why not? Digital imaging is personal, it's creative, and it's easily within your grasp. Here's what each chapter of this book will show you.

- **Chapter 1.** How Do I Get My Pictures in There? You don't necessarily need a scanner or digital camera to get your pictures into your computer. This chapter covers all the ways to do it, then introduces you to image files and how they work.

- **Chapter 2.** Sharing Pictures with Friends, Family, and Online Pals. Once you've got the hang of going digital, you'll need the right tools to be able to send and receive pictures. This chapter will introduce you to the Picture Gallery and tell you all about messages, e-mail, digital postcards, digital photo albums, *and* AOL forums and sites where you can download digital pictures.

- **Chapter 3.** All Those Special Memories: Creating Simple Photo Albums and Other Keepsakes. In this chapter we'll teach you how to design your own online family album with photographs, captions, special fonts, and clip art. There's no better way to personalize your memories. You'll also get hints about how to turn your photographs into unique, personalized gifts such as calendars, mugs, and T-shirts.

- **Chapter 4.** Family Trees and Other Personal Records. Did you ever have to draw a family tree for a school project? Remember getting your parents to jog their memories for the people and the dates that make up your personal history? Well, now you can embellish the nostalgia of that simple chart with photographs and personal, quirky sidelights, and even get help tracing your ancestors online. But why stop there? Plenty of other projects lend themselves to digital pictures, such as taking a property inventory and assembling a photographic address book or recipe book.

- **Chapter 5.** The Great Photo Swap: Posting Pictures for Mates, Dates, and Online Buddies. Looking for love in all the wrong places? Or just curious to make some new friends who share your interests? Pin up a photo and a zippy bio of yourself online. This chapter shows you how.

- **Chapter 6.** Celebrating! Invitations, Announcements, and Other Ways to Spread Good News. Wouldn't it be fun to send a New Year's Eve party invitation that plays "Auld Lang Syne"? You can. Check out this chapter for more great ideas and step-by-step instructions.

- **Chapter 7.** Creating Web Pages with Personal Publisher. Personal Publisher lets you create your very own Web page with all kinds of animated images and background sounds. Learn all the insider's tips on how to express yourself.

- **Chapter 8.** Kids and Digital Pictures. Find out how your kids can use digital pictures for schoolwork, for creative projects, and just for fun. It's a great opportunity to work on something together. This chapter tells you everything you need to know, including how to control what they get exposed to online.

- **Chapter 9.** Using Digital Pictures at Work. If you run a small business, you can use digital pictures in all kinds of innovative ways: Create and distribute online catalogs and promotional materials, track product inventory, and maintain client contacts. Find out how.

- **Chapter 10.** How to Set Up a Home Digital Lab. If you get serious about digital pictures, consider setting up a home digital lab. It's fun, and a lot less messy than an old-fashioned darkroom. You will be surprised at how easy and inexpensive it is.

- **Chapter 11.** The Power of Graphics Software. The real trick to success with digital lies in having the right images and software. Once you're clued in, you'll be able to download all kinds of great pictures—not to mention ordering software and art files straight from the AOL Store.

- **Chapter 12.** Touching Up and Improving Pictures. Whether you're a professional or amateur photographer, this chapter can help you make the most of your digital pictures. It's filled with invaluable tips and insider advice.

- **Chapter 13.** Advanced Imaging and Special Effects. Learn the secrets of the imaging pros. This chapter introduces you to more advanced topics, like importing, resizing, and cropping pictures, along with color correction and creating special effects. You'll also learn about AOL forums where members exchange information about images and consult with the experts.

- **Chapter 14.** Graphics and Multimedia Online. Once you've mastered the art and science of digital pictures, read this chapter to add sound, video, and other multimedia effects.

- **Chapter 15.** Storing and Keeping Track of Pictures. The online community swaps pictures like crazy. But there will come a time when you want to organize all those digital gems to print them out and enjoy. This chapter shows you how.

What You Need

You need to know a thing or two about how we wrote this book. With all those different types of computers out there, we thought it would be best to keep the instructions simple. So we're assuming your computer has the Windows 95 operating system. But you should be able to follow along without any trouble if you've got another operating system, including one created for the Macintosh. You should also know that the book was written to help you make the most of the features available in version 4.0 of AOL. You may find that some of the AOL keywords or Web addresses will change over time. And you may even find that your screen looks slightly different from the screen shots that have been used to illustrate this book. That's because the service is always being updated and improved.

Images online are the most exciting development we've seen in a long time. This book will open your eyes to the many ways you can use them. What are you waiting for?

PART I

Everyday Graphics on AOL

WHERE TO JOIN THE DIGITAL IMAGING CROWD

If you've been standing on the sidelines because you're afraid of the term "digital imaging," it's time to demystify the whole process. It's really all about getting your favorite pictures on your computer, where you can use them and display them proudly. No fancy technology, no special training. Just start, as you always do, by bringing a roll of film to the photo shop. Then join your friends who are swapping pictures on the AOL service.

1

HOW DO I GET MY PICTURES IN THERE?

There's no big mystery to getting your favorite pictures online. And the sooner you figure out how to do it, the sooner you can start enjoying the creativity and fun digital imaging has to offer. Let's begin by introducing you to the ways you can get your pictures "in there" and the different digital picture file formats you might come across.

Yes, you can have it all. Digital pictures are both fun *and* practical. Digital pictures offer the following advantages:

- **Convenience.** With digital pictures, you can get more copies any time you want. You can also crop, resize, and retouch photographs without having to send them to the lab.

- **Usefulness.** Once you get used to digital pictures, you'll wonder how you ever did without them. You can use them for holiday and birthday cards, a household property inventory, business presentations, school reports ... the list goes on and on. Best of all, it's easy to share them with other people online.

- **Savings.** In the long run (and even the short run) it costs less to produce digital pictures. Once you have a scan or CD made, or purchase a digital camera, you can create different versions of the same pictures over and over again.

- **Fun.** Sure digital pictures have practical advantages. But we like them because they're *fun*.

10

Getting Digital Pictures

First things first. You already have hundreds of downloadable images online right now: clip art, nature images, cartoons, and more, and you can scan them. It's also easy *and* inexpensive to convert your own rolls of film and existing photographs into digital pictures at a film lab, or take them with a digital camera or on your video camera. Here's how:

Download Them

To find images that can be downloaded (downloadable images), go to picture areas like the Photography Forum (keyword: **Photography Forum**), the Image Exchange (keyword: **Imageex**), and Pictures (keyword: **Pictures**). We'll cover others at the end of chapter 2. Or you can visit your favorite AOL forums and channels like Entertainment, Travel, and Sports. You'll find plenty of digital pictures in your areas of interest.

Take Them to a Digital Lab

Most film labs can put the pictures on your rolls of film or negatives on a floppy disk or photo CD-ROM. This takes about the same amount of time and costs about the same amount of money as developing prints. Simply check off the photo CD option when you fill out the form. When the pictures are ready, slip the disk into your computer and launch the Picture Gallery on the AOL service. From there, you can view and save photos to your hard drive, convert them, and work with them.

Scan Them

You can also scan existing photographs and artwork, or have them scanned for you and saved onto a disk. A scanner is a device that copies your pictures into a computer. Maybe you know someone with access to one (they can start under $100). If not, take your artwork to a copy shop that offers graphics services, like Kinko's, and have them scan it for you and give you the file on a disk.

A copy shop should be able to scan an image for you within 24 hours for under $15. That's sort of expensive, but it might be worthwhile for special objects, like your college diploma or your watercolor collection. If you didn't take the photograph or create the artwork yourself, most copy shops also require a signed permission form from the photographer or artist. Check around and see if a photo processing lab can scan your prints for less. Some charge only $3 to $10 per print, plus a charge for the disk, while others might charge a flat fee of around $25 for 24 exposures.

Use a Digital Camera

You can also try using a digital camera. It's fun, convenient, and way more affordable than it used to be. With a digital camera, you can take photos the same as you would with a regular camera, but without film. It records the images automatically into a digital format. You can then load the files from the digital camera straight into your computer. Like regular cameras, digital cameras only let you take a certain number of pictures before you have to unload the "film." When the digital camera is full, you simply plug it into the serial port on

QUESTIONS TO ASK PHOTO DEVELOPING LABS

- Can you convert photos or film to digital format?
- What digital format do you use?
- Can you format files as GIFs or JPEGs?
- How much does it cost to copy my files to disks?
- How many pictures can you fit on a disk?
- How much does it cost to convert my files to CDs?
- How many rolls of film can you fit on a CD?
- How long does it take?
- Can I get a rush order and what is the extra cost?
- Can I use the same CD later to add more images?
- Do you convert images in-house or do you send the pictures or roll of film out?
- Do you guarantee your services?
- Can I furnish my own blank disks or CDs?

11

your computer. Fortunately, it only takes a few minutes to load the images onto your computer and then you can start all over again.

Imagine never having to pay to develop a roll of film again! Chapters 10 and 12 help you select a digital camera and use it to take quality digital pictures. You can also find great deals through the AOL Store's Digital Shop (figure 1.1) from vendors such as Casio and Minolta.

Use Your Video Camera

Do you have a video camera? Do you know you can use it to take digital pictures? Professionals use an expensive video card and software. If you're like the rest of us, you will do just fine using Play Incorporated's Snappy, a nifty piece of hardware selling for about $200. Simply attach one end to your printer port and the other end to your video camera, VCR, or television. It displays frames from your videos so you can select the good ones and save them as digital pictures. You can have a blast creating a show for your family and friends: wedding scenes, reunions, whitewater rafting adventures. Find out more about cameras and accessories at the Digital Shop (keyword: **Digital Shop**) under Cameras & Video Hardware. Stop by to check out digital video cameras that plug right into your computer, from vendors such as Casio, Minolta, and Kodak.

Digital Picture File Formats

You'll get the best results if you understand a thing or two about file formats. Don't be scared off by the technical-sounding names. All you need to know is that digital pictures are like ordinary photographs and graphics—only you have to either create them on a computer or convert them to a format that the computer can read. Digital pictures come in several different file formats—which are indicated by a filename

FIGURE 1.2
Continuous tone photograph

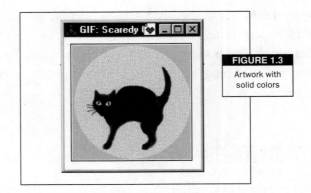

FIGURE 1.3
Artwork with
solid colors

extension (such as GIF, JPEG, or BMP). Filename extensions tell your computer what application to launch the file with and indicate the format in which the picture was saved. All these filename extensions may look like alphabet soup, but you will get to know their differences and the advantages and disadvantages of each.

Digital pictures come in the following flavors:

- JPEG: Small file sizes, high image quality, and short download times have made JPEGs (pronounced jay-peg) popular both on and off the Web. The JPEG file format is ideal for detailed, continuous tone photographs like the one shown in figure 1.2. JPEG files work well online because anyone can view them with a Web browser. (JPEG stands for Joint Photographic Experts Group, the organization that developed this file format.)

- GIF: The GIF file format enjoys many of the JPEG's advantages. However, it lends itself better to artwork with solid colors, like the drawing shown in figure 1.3, than to photographs. You can also do neat things with GIFs—like assemble a few of them into animations, or eliminate the background color to make them blend seamlessly with a Web page. (GIF stands for Graphic Interchange Format. People used this file format to share digital pictures on online services before the Web existed.)

- BMP: Windows users often exchange BMP files because Microsoft Windows' built-in Paint program can open them. In addition, most applications can handle the BMP (bitmap) file format, which works well for photographs.

14

- Other image formats: In addition to the common file formats listed above, you might run into digital pictures created in popular graphics applications or those used by graphics professionals. These include TIF, EPS, PCX, PCT, and WMF files, which you can learn about in the many graphics forums on the AOL service. You can open many different picture file formats in AOL 4.0. Simply select File, Open from the task bar at the top of the screen.

When to Use Which File Format

Now that you know about all the various digital picture formats, how do you figure out when to use what? You can convert and save to different graphic file formats with the Picture Gallery. Which image file format you choose depends on how you plan to use your digital pictures. Keep in mind that you can convert high-density images to low-density, but not vice versa.

The following list tells you what digital picture file formats work best for which purpose:

- GIF and JPEG: In most cases, you can't go wrong with GIFs and JPEGs. Use them for your Web page or any online communications. Web browsers only support the GIF and JPEG formats. Files saved in these formats also transfer quickly when e-mailing or uploading. But keep in mind that many applications—such as word processing, page layout, spreadsheet, and presentation programs—can't handle GIFs and JPEGs. (AOL 4.0 *can*.)

WHICH IS BETTER, GIF OR JPEG?

GIF and JPEG are popular because most Web browsers support them. But when do you use a GIF and when do you use a JPEG? The following lists can help you determine how to format your digital pictures:

GIF	JPEG
Line art	Scanned photos
Cartoons	Full-color images
Bold colors	Photo-realistic images
Icons	Gray-scale images
Bold lines	Complex color gradients
Large areas of solid color	Detailed shading

15

USES FOR DIGITAL PICTURES

You probably already have lots of ideas about how to use your digital pictures. But here are a few that you may not have thought of yet. Throughout this book you'll find more.

- Illustrate flyers and brochures.
- Personalize letters and e-mail.
- Create multimedia slide shows.
- Publish an online newsletter.
- Create a Web page.
- Spruce up school reports and assignments.
- Illustrate a family tree.
- Assemble an online photo album.
- Create an illustrated calendar.

16

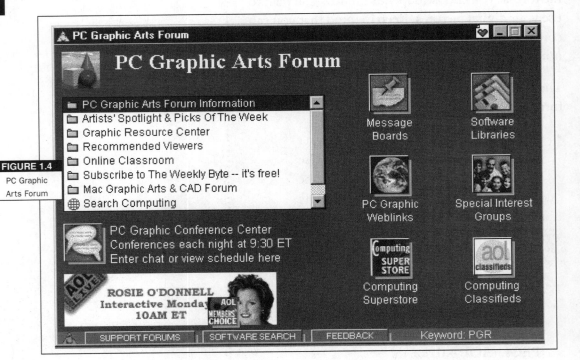

FIGURE 1.4

PC Graphic
Arts Forum

- BMP: Use when exchanging files with Windows users who might want to use the files in documents that were created in other applications. Just about every Windows application can handle BMPs. Many of the Macintosh applications can import BMPs too. But keep in mind: Macintosh users may not be able to look at your file before importing it into a document.

See? No more alphabet soup. Now that you know a little about file formats, you can send a cyberbouquet of roses or ogle Uncle Harry's new fireplace. You can learn even more about digital pictures and graphics terms at the PC Graphic Arts Forum (keyword: **Graphics**), as shown in figure 1.4.

So Now You've Got Your Image File

Once you have your digital pictures, the fun can really begin. E-mail them to relatives and friends, upload them to forums, use them for all kinds of creative projects, or just keep them for yourself. You can even make a slide show presentation out of them that will also work as a screen saver for your computer. The possibilities are endless.

17

Chapter 2 will introduce you to the Picture Gallery, AOL's built-in tool kit that gives you everything you need to store and craft your favorite pictures. And don't forget—you can *manipulate* your digital pictures. Change your eye color, crop out your blind date, even add special effects like textured backgrounds and negative images. So knock yourself out. Make your peonies look like they nabbed the blue ribbon, or draw a mustache and horns on your boss. Chapter 11 discusses imaging and graphics software further, so you can put what's in your head on your screen.

AOL Channels and forums give you just about everything you need to become a digital picture whiz. Visit the Pictures area (keyword: **Pictures**) of the Interests channel for ideas and tips. You can even enter a digital picture contest! It's time to get rolling with all those pictures.

MINIMUM SYSTEM REQUIREMENTS FOR AOL 4.0

Windows 95 and Windows 98
- 16 megabytes RAM system configuration
- Pentium-class PC
- 45 megabytes available hard disk space
- 640 x 480, 256 colors screen resolution, or better
- 14.4 Kbps modem, or faster

Windows 3.1
- 16 megabytes RAM system configuration
- 486-class PC, or better
- 30 megabytes available hard disk space
- 640 x 480, 256 colors screen resolution, or better
- 14.4 Kbps modem, or faster

Macintosh
- 12 megabytes RAM system configuration
- System 7.1, or better
- 68040 or PowerPC Macintosh
- 640 x 480, 256 colors display, or better
- 14.4 Kbps modem, or faster

If you need to upgrade any system components, be sure to visit AOL's Hardware Shop at keyword **Hardware Center**. (See the Upgrade Tips section.) Users with Windows 95 machines that don't meet the AOL 4.0 for Windows 95 requirements can use the 16-bit version (the version which is normally used on Windows 3.1).

2

SHARING PICTURES WITH FRIENDS, FAMILY, AND ONLINE PALS

ere's the part you've been waiting for: how to play around with pictures and special backgrounds in your e-mail, Instant Messages, online postcards, and Address Book. You're going to love the Picture Gallery, which is built into AOL 4.0; it makes viewing, editing, and swapping pictures on the AOL service easier than flipping through a photo album. We'll also show you how to add to your collection with the large and varied assortment of pictures you can download. Finally, we'll help you put together a simple multimedia presentation that documents your newborn's coming home from the hospital, for example.

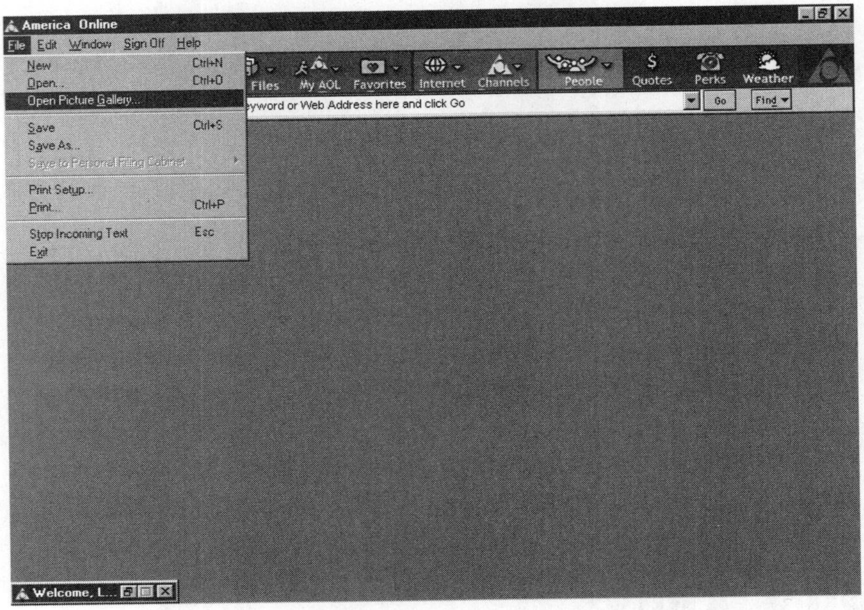

FIGURE 2.1

Select Open
Picture Gallery

Using the Picture Gallery

The Picture Gallery is your premier tool for managing and manipulating digital pictures. You can use the directory feature to find and organize picture files on your hard drive or disk, use the thumbnail feature to preview miniature versions of your pictures, use the toolbar to change the full-size version of the picture and place it right in an e-mail message or other document.

To launch the Picture Gallery:

1. Select Open Picture Gallery from the File menu (see figure 2.1). You'll see the Open Picture Gallery dialogue box (see figure 2.2).

2. Browse for the directory folder, disk, or CD-ROM that contains your digital picture files.

3. Select the file and click on Open Gallery. The Picture Gallery dialogue box appears, as shown in figure 2.3. You can either place the image in a file or e-mail, or view and edit it using the toolbar buttons.

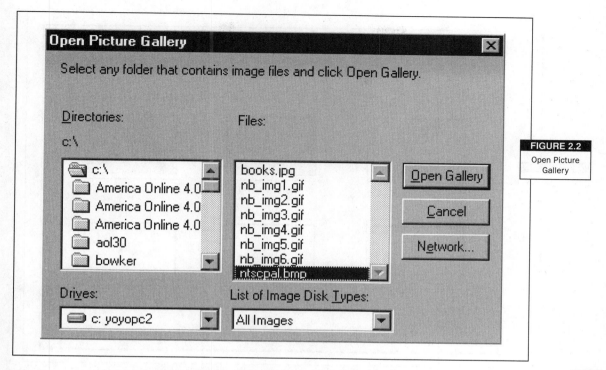

FIGURE 2.2

Open Picture Gallery

See how easy it is? The Picture Gallery dialogue box displays miniature versions of your pictures, called "thumbnails." It can show six pictures at a time. Click on Next to view more.

Placing Pictures in Messages and Files

The Picture Gallery dialogue box makes it easy to place your 25th anniversary party photo into an e-mail or special picture file. But before you do, remember the discussion on file formats in chapter 1. You may want to open your picture first and save it to an appropriate file format. The next section, "Touching Up, Saving, and Converting Picture Files," tells you how.

To place your picture into a message or file:

1. Open a document or create a new message, then display the Picture Gallery dialogue box.

2. Click on the photo and drag the image into your message or file.

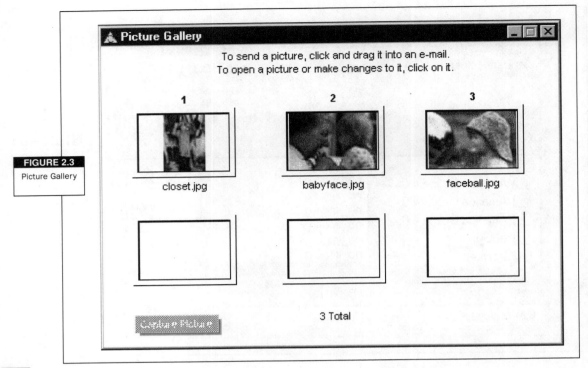

FIGURE 2.3

Picture Gallery

Touching Up, Saving, and Converting Picture Files

The Picture Gallery also provides you with an image editing window, as shown in figure 2.4. The image editing window displays your image at actual size and includes tools for retouching. For example, you can crop the 25th anniversary picture to eliminate the caterer's elbow and rotate it on an angle for a more interesting layout. This section explains the image editing window tools, and tells you how to save and convert your images.

You can also convert images to different file formats. But remember that images with fewer colors, higher compression levels, and lower resolutions do not convert successfully to image formats with more colors, lower compression levels, or higher resolutions. For example, you gain nothing from converting a GIF into a JPEG, though some JPEGs can work well as GIFs. The GIF format only supports 256 colors, while the JPEG format supports millions of colors.

To display an image in the image editing window:

1. Display your thumbnails in the Picture Gallery dialogue box.

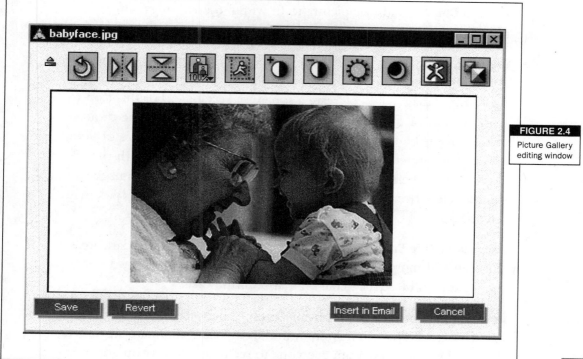

FIGURE 2.4

Picture Gallery
editing window

23

2. Select the picture you want to edit by clicking on it.

3. Begin touching it up.

You can click on different toolbar buttons to edit your digital pictures. The toolbar buttons are located at the top of the image editing window below the title bar. If you need to be reminded what each button does, simply glide your cursor over it to see a brief pop-up description. If you can't find the toolbar buttons, click on the down arrow to reveal them.

- **Rotate Picture.** Rotates the picture in 90 degree increments so you can make jazzy layouts.

- **Flip Picture Horizontally.** Flips the picture backwards along the Y axis (left or right).

- **Flip Picture Vertically.** Flips the picture upside down along the X axis (top or bottom).

- **Zoom In/Out.** Expands the picture to fit within the viewing format. This may distort your image.

- **Cropping.** Crops your picture to a defined area, to eliminate part of the image. To define your cropping area, place your cursor on the image, then drag it diagonally to create a square or rectangle. For this icon to work, you must first select the area you want to crop. Say the choicest picture from the anniversary party is marred by the presence of your ubiquitous caterer. Place your cursor on the picture and, with the left mouse button held down, drag a box around the part of the image you want to keep. Everything *outside* that box, including the chief cook, will bite the dust.

- **Increase Picture Contrast.** Intensifies your picture's light and dark areas. This can add more definition to photographs that look washed out or too dark. Don't lose the detail on that beautiful cake.

- **Decrease Picture Contrast.** Decreases contrast between the picture's light and dark areas. This can help smooth the edges and eliminate unwanted details. (Do you really want everyone to see that blemish you got right before the party?)

- **Brighten Picture.** Brightens a picture that looks too dark.

- **Dim Picture.** Darkens a picture that looks too light.

- **Invert Picture.** Creates a "negative" of the current picture. This reverses all of the colors as well as the light and dark areas. You can use these negative images to add interesting effects to your layouts.

- **Convert Picture to Grayscale.** Makes a color image look like a black-and-white photograph. Turning a picture into a grayscale image can reduce its file size, and shows you how the image would look when printed on a black-and-white printer. Grayscale can also give your pictures an interesting "old-fashioned" look.

The image editing window also has a button bar below the picture for additional tasks:

- **Save.** Saves the image.

24

- **Revert.** Reverts to the last version of the image saved and eliminates all edits made up to that point. When experimenting, the Revert button is your friend.

- **Insert in E-mail.** Inserts the current image in the currently open e-mail message.

- **Cancel.** Cancels the last change made or gives you the option to save it and then returns you to the Picture Gallery. To save your changes:

1. Select Save As from the File menu. The Save Graphic As dialogue box will appear.

2. Select a folder from the Save In: list.

3. Enter a name for your file in the File name: text field.

4. Use the File Types list to select the format if you want to convert your file. For more about file formats, see chapter 1.

5. Click on Save.

Jazzing Up E-Mail Messages

Sure, you can use the Picture Gallery's Insert in E-mail feature to do just that. But it is just as easy to start from the Write Mail screen (click on Write on the AOL toolbar or enter Control-M), where you can add snazzy backgrounds or embed pictures

IMAGE AND BACKGROUND TIPS FOR E-MAIL

Have fun using pictures and images in your e-mail messages. Follow these tips to get the best results:

- **Choose appropriate background and text colors.** Business messages should look professional and low-key. You can use more casual color schemes with friends and family.

- **Watch your colors.** Use light-colored text on dark-colored backgrounds and vice versa. Otherwise, people may have trouble reading your messages.

- **Watch your file sizes.** Embedded and background images increase your e-mail message's file size, and can slow down your transmission time.

25

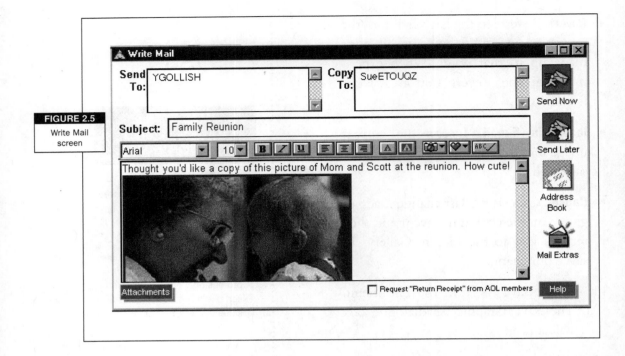

FIGURE 2.5
Write Mail screen

right in the message (instead of using an attachment), as shown in figure 2.5. This is a great way to share pictures with other AOL members—although your friends on the Internet may not be able to see them.

Right Click with your mouse where you want to insert a digital picture. When the pop-up menu appears, select the Insert a Picture option. When the Open dialogue box appears, you can browse for the picture you want and select it. That's it.

To add a patterned image to the background of your e-mail message:

1. Place your cursor anywhere in your e-mail message and click on it with the right mouse button.

2. When the pop-up menu appears, click on the Background Picture option. The Open dialogue box will appear.

3. Browse for a background image, then click on Open.

Hint: Image backgrounds work best when you use subtle patterns with low contrast levels. You don't want your friends to have to squint and sweat trying to read your black letters against a fuchsia background.

To add a solid-colored background to an e-mail message:

1. Place your cursor anywhere in your e-mail message and click on it with the right mouse button.

2. When the pop-up menu appears, click on the Background Color option with the right mouse button. The color palette dialogue box will appear.

TIPS FOR SENDING AND RECEIVING FILES

The most common way to send a file is as an attachment via e-mail. Now, with AOL's version 4.0, you can send digital pictures through e-mail.

When you're sending and receiving files online, there are a few things you need to keep in mind:

1. When sending documents of any type it is better to send a text-only file. These files are often referred to as ASCII files. They are straight text files with no fancy printer codes, no special formatting. These files can be read by any computer and any word processing program. They can also be read by cross-platform computers, which means that if you're on a PC and send to someone on a Mac, that person can still read your file.

2. Size becomes very important when you're sending or receiving files. Bigger is not better in this instance. When at all possible, compress large files. Note that AOL 4.0 will compress multiple attached files when you send a message. If you don't already have a program to zip and unzip files, you should get one. (One of the most popular and best programs is called WinZip.) For more information about working within compressed files on the AOL service, go to Member Services (keyword: **Member Services**).

3. Never accept files from someone you don't know. A nasty virus could take down your computer. Or you could get a picture you'd rather not see or rather not have your children see.

4. Never send attachments to e-mail lists. Some people are billed by the size of the files they receive and won't appreciate your sending them an unsolicited attachment. Some people just prefer not to receive unasked-for files from others. Some don't know how to (or can't) open attachments. To these people, your attachment is not only unwanted but useless. Lastly, not everyone uses the same type of computer—some are on Macs and some are on PCs—nor do they all have the same operating systems or the same programs. Your attachment will be nothing but a nuisance in such cases.

5. Your modem's speed makes all the difference in the world—especially when it comes to sending and receiving images. So consider upgrading, if you are not already using a 56 Kbps modem. The Modem Shop, part of the AOL Store (keyword: **Modem Shop** or **AOL Store**) includes a great selection of modems from top vendors including U.S. Robotics.

3. Pick your favorite among the variety of colors, click on it, then click on the OK button.

AOL Online Greetings

What's a long-distance relationship without postcards? That's what we thought. You'll be happy to know that Online Greetings (keyword: **Online Greetings**) offers a great assortment of ready-made pictures to choose from, like the one in figure 2.6. A package of ten cards will cost you about five dollars. Once you purchase them, you must use them within 90 days. AOL reminds you every time you send one, and tells you how many you have left. They'll also give a holler as the expiration date approaches. The Online Greetings area also offers Slideshow Greetings and animated greetings.

To purchase your greetings:

1. Browse the categories and greetings.

2. Select the greeting by doubleclicking on it

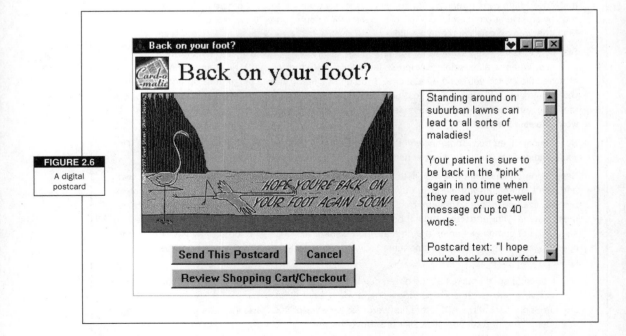

FIGURE 2.6

A digital postcard

3. Type the screen name or e-mail address, subject line, and message.

4. Click on Send.

5. Enter credit card information, as requested, and click on OK.

When your friends send you greetings, why not save them to a file in the Picture Gallery so you can create a personalized collection? You could use them to eventually put together a "through the years" scrapbook. Or reuse the images in some of your special projects in part II of this book. Make your own tradition.

Adding Pictures to Your Address Book

Are you wondering what your new online buddy, SueETOUQZ looks like? Ask her to send you a picture, and save it to your Address Book which you can get to from the Mail Center icon on the AOL toolbar (keyword: **Mail**).

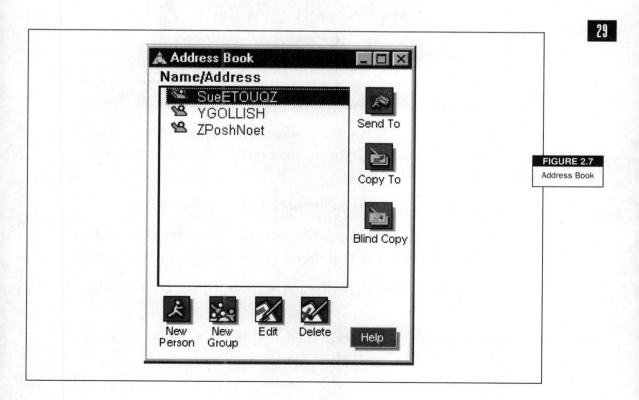

FIGURE 2.7
Address Book

FIGURE 2.8

Picture box

To add a picture to go with a contact's name in your Address Book:

1. Go to the Mail Center (keyword: **Mail**) and select the Address Book from the Mail menu. You'll see the Address Book window, as shown in figure 2.7.

2. Select a screen name from your list of buddies and click on Edit.

3. When the Edit Person dialogue box appears, click on the Picture tab. You will get the Picture box, as shown in figure 2.8.

4. Click on the Select Picture button and select the picture file from your directory.

5. If you want, click on the Person tab to update the profile information, or click on OK.

You can also add new contacts by clicking on New Person and entering the information when the New Person dialogue box appears.

AOL Picture Libraries

Supplement your own digital picture library with images already online. Most AOL forums have areas for downloading and posting files—including pictures—so members can exchange information and get to know each other better. Insiders know where to go for the prime pickings. Try these:

The Gallery

Start your search for digital pictures with a visit to the AOL Portrait Gallery (keyword: **Gallery**). The Gallery has various areas for downloading, viewing, and posting pictures. You can browse the AOL Member Portrait Gallery for pictures of your online buddies and add a picture of yourself, or visit the Rogue Gallery and see what your hosts at AOL look like. The Family Album features pictures of AOL members with—you guessed it—their families, and also encourages members to post. To submit pictures to the AOL Member Portrait Gallery or the Family Album, just follow the instructions posted in the Gallery area (in the Frequently Asked Questions area).

But you can do a lot more than just take a gander at your friends. Try some of these activities:

- Make a photo album: Have you made new friends in the chat groups you frequent? Make a photo album of all the people in a chat group, upload it to the forum's posting area, and invite everyone to take a look at it.

- Publish a book: Create a booklet of useful things you've learned in your favorite forums for other members to use as a reference. Give forum members credit for the information they've provided and include their photographs.

- Add pictures to your Web site: Create a Web page with photographs of your favorite AOL friends (make sure you get their permission). Add links to their Web pages. Chapter 7 gives more details about setting up a Web page.

HOW DIGITAL PICTURES CAN HELP YOUR BUSINESS

Sure, you can have fun with digital pictures. But they're more than a toy. Digital pictures can also help you generate customers for your small business. Begin by using digital pictures in simple ways that don't require a lot of time and effort. As you grow more comfortable with them, digital pictures can also become part of your long-term projects.

Digital pictures can help your business in the following ways:

- **Personalize your communications.** You can send messages including your logo and contact information—think of it as your online letterhead. Or you can send personalized postcards and messages to clients for holidays, to acknowledge important events in their lives, to wish them well, and to make announcements.

- **Keep track of contacts.** Your Address Book helps you keep track of clients, colleagues, and that new contact you made at a conference last week. You can place a photograph or company logo with each person's contact information to jog your memory when you address a message to them.

- **Promote your products and services.** Build a Web page, set up a downloadable slide presentation, or create an online catalog. You can even develop an attractive online publication to keep customers up-to-date on your latest sales, celebrations, and other events. For small businesses, the AOL service and the Internet can help you reach more people for less money. (AOL's Prime Host Service provides a full-featured Web site solution, all under one storefront.) For large business, online communications make it easy to update your printed materials and tide you over until the next press run.

- **Create a company newsletter.** If you and your coworkers work from different locations, an online newsletter can build a sense of teamwork and morale. It will keep everyone up-to-date and help colleagues put faces to the people they communicate with by phone or e-mail every day. Best of all, online newsletters are cheaper than the printed kind.

- **And more...** Take pictures of your inventory and put them online (many database programs let you incorporate digital pictures) so people can track it more easily. Develop online training materials that reduce training costs and increase productivity. For example, a slide presentation or a Web page "Help" area can guide your coworkers through common tasks, like doing a mail merge.

ClickArt

Sure, "a picture is worth a thousand words." But sometimes a photograph says too *much* when you'd prefer something sleek and simple. In that case, stop by the ClickArt area (keyword: **ClickArt**). You'll find lots of sample spot illustrations—

where else can you turn when you simply must have a picture of a walrus in a top hat?—but you can also find great deals on click art collections. The collection offers a variety of styles, so it's a great place to look, whether your project or message is business-like, casual, cutting-edge, or formal. It is especially useful for:

- Online stationery and logos

- Navigation buttons on your Web pages

- Decorative art for newsletters

The Internet

To tap into the many image collections available on the Internet, click on the Internet toolbar button (the globe), and then on Go to the Web to jump to the home page of the AOL service. From there, you can enter a keyword (such as **Images** or **Gallery** in the AOL NetFind text field) and click on Find. Be smart about your search terms (be specific) to avoid an unmanageable number of hits. When the list of links appears, read the information and visit the sites that appeal to you.

Images in the Public Domain Online

33

Not all the photos and images you find on the AOL service or Web sites are there for the taking. If they're copyrighted, you can't use them unless you get permission from the owner, or purchase the right to use them. Under current copyright laws, an author or artist's work is automatically copyrighted for the duration of the person's life, plus 50 years. After that, the work becomes part of the public domain.

You can use public domain pictures freely, without worrying about copyright infringement. To find public domain graphics on the Internet, use AOL NetFind to search for something like **Public Domain Photographs**. Many people also offer public domain graphics on their personal Web sites. Try the Icon Bazaar at http://www.iconbazaar.com.

Commercial Digital Pictures

If you're looking for stock photos or a collection of related images, consider buying a CD-ROM from the ClickArt area (keyword: **ClickArt**). Once you buy a clip art or stock photography collection, you can use the images as often as you want.

Taking Stock

You've come a long way from feeling clueless about digital images. Now you know how to get them on your machine, convert them to the proper file format, and store and use them in the Picture Gallery. You created a slide show and sent pictures by e-mail and Instant Messages. Maybe you're even sending postcards regularly. But the best part about pictures is they help you be creative—and that's what you'll learn how to do next, in part II.

PART II

The Digital Picture Idea Book

Here comes the creative part. You've gathered all your favorite digital pictures together in the Picture Gallery, and you know how to personalize them and send them to practically anyone online. Now it's time to express your personality with pictures. Even if you feel like you've got the skill of a five-year-old with scissors and paste, you'll find the tools online that make it possible to create masterpieces you can be proud of. This section will lead you through six easy activities: creating a photo album, building a family tree, posting a personal profile to meet mates and dates, making invitations and announcements, creating a Web page, and helping your kids get the most out of digital imaging. We'll also whet your appetite with creative suggestions for other projects, because once you get going with digital pictures you won't want to stop.

3

ALL THOSE SPECIAL MEMORIES: CREATING SIMPLE PHOTO ALBUMS AND OTHER KEEPSAKES

Everyone's got a box of pictures to organize in an album "someday." Or maybe you've already discovered the pleasure of arranging your collection and dressing it up with stickers, quotations, funny quips, and scraps of your favorite treasures. This type of personalization barely touches the surface of what is possible when you create a photo album online. You already know how to enhance your pictures with cropping, touching up, and highlighting. But there is much more—your creativity in assembling and describing them is limited only by your imagination. And you never have to worry about faded, torn, or lost photos.

This chapter takes you through the process of putting together a simple album to commemorate your child's first haircut. But you can use the same skills to make greeting cards, notepads, calendars, and all kinds of other creative projects.

So let's get started. But be more creative than you might be in a standard album. Arrange the pictures in unusual configurations. Add captions and flattering backgrounds. Pick a theme you can elaborate with special fonts and add decorative touches.

Suppose you just took little Eddie for his first real haircut and brought home "before" and "after" pictures of his lustrous mop. Instead of merely placing the two pictures side by side on a page, why not set up a whole barber shop theme? Download a picture of an old-time barber's chair and crop Eddie's picture so it looks like he's sitting in it. (If you make a mistake, no big deal; just start over with a fresh backup copy of the file.) Add some clip art of a barber's pole and even put a scanned image of the newly clipped hair at the bottom. You get the idea. Suddenly you have way more than a page from a standard photo album.

It doesn't matter what theme you choose: vacation highlights, pets, college memories, even your salt and pepper shaker collection. Let's take it step by step.

Gathering Your Pictures

To begin making your digital photo album, gather together the electronic pictures you want to use. Whether they're on CD-ROMs, disks, or in the Picture Gallery, copy them into a single folder. Give the folder a name—for example, "Eddie's First Haircut." If you prefer, you can preview thumbnails of all the pictures in the Picture Gallery, then open those you want to use in the image editing window. Save them to your photo album folder.

To select images in the Picture Gallery:

1. Select Open Picture Gallery from the File menu (see figure 3.1).

2. When the Open Picture Gallery dialogue box appears, browse for the folder, disk, or CD-ROM containing the digital pictures you want (see figure 3.2).

3. When the Files list appears, click on Open Gallery. Peruse the collection, and select the best pictures for your new album.

4. Select a picture by clicking on it. The image will appear in the image editing window.

5. Click on Save As in the File menu. When the Save Graphic As dialogue box appears, browse for your folder, name the file, and click on Save again. You can also convert your image to a different file format by selecting an option from the File Type list.

6. Then click on Save.

Touching Them Up

Now that you've gathered all the best shots of your little darling with and without his tresses, look them over and see if any could use a little touching up. You can also edit your digital pictures on the fly as you select and place them into your photo album file. Is Eddie's face in shadow? Is the barber's white coat causing too much glare? The image editing window gives you an assortment of tools for making your photographs look just the way you want them to.

39

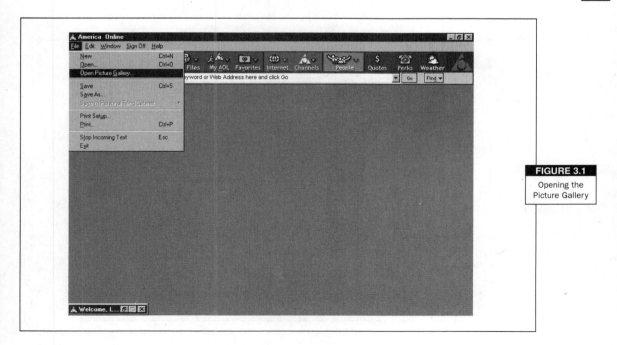

FIGURE 3.1

Opening the Picture Gallery

40

Display the thumbnails in the Picture Gallery dialogue box and select the picture you want to edit. When the image editing window appears, as shown in figure 3.3, make changes by clicking on the toolbar. (Chapter 2 explains in detail what each toolbar button does.) Remember toolbar button reminders appear when you pass your cursor over the icons.

Feel free to experiment. If you don't like the results, click on Revert to return to the last saved version of your picture. To avoid frustration and heartbreak, save your file whenever you like a change you just made.

Creating a Photo Album File

To create a new file for the photo album:

1. Select New from the File menu. The blank editing window will open.

2. Select Open Picture Gallery from the File menu. The Open Picture Gallery dialogue box appears. (Or, you can click on the Camera in the blank editing window and select Insert A Picture. Browse for the file with your photo, doubleclick on it, and it will appear in your new photo album file.)

3. Browse for your photo album folder. When you find it, you'll see the list of files displayed in the Files list.

4. Click on Open Gallery. The Open Pictures dialogue box will appear with thumbnails of your pictures.

TEN TIPS FOR THE PERFECT DIGITAL ALBUM

The following tips can help you create a digital photo album that your friends and family will enjoy looking at for years to come.

1. Choose pictures with a common theme.

2. Use sharp, clear pictures, or touch them up until they are.

3. Use both vertically and horizontally oriented pictures for more interesting compositions.

4. Label each photograph with a caption.

5. Use humor—everyone loves to laugh.

6. Use background and text colors that highlight your album and pictures.

7. Use pictures of different sizes to add variety to the layout.

8. Edit pictures in the image editing window before adding them to your photo album.

9. Crop out unnecessary or unwanted areas to make your subjects stand out more.

10. Use only a few pictures for each album so others can download and view them quickly.

41

5. Select a picture and then click on it, drag, and drop the picture into your photo album file.

6. Select Save As from the File menu. The Save As dialogue box appears.

7. Choose a name.

8. Click on Save.

To enter text:

1. Place your cursor where you want to enter the text.

2. Begin typing.

3. Select the text by placing your cursor at the beginning of the line, holding down your mouse key, and dragging it to the end of the line.

4. Select a font from the pull-down font list.

5. Select a font size from the pull-down size list.

6. Use the toolbar buttons to format your text. Hint: Sometimes less is more! If there is an existing text file that you want to insert, click on the camera in the blank editing window and select Insert Text File. Locate the file in Open Text File and doubleclick on it. It will then appear in your photo file.

To add a background color:

1. Click on the A symbol with the blue background. The Color Palette dialogue box appears.

2. Select a color and click on OK to return to the text editing window.

To add a patterned background image:

1. Click on the Camera and select Background Picture.

2. When the Open dialogue box displays, browse for a folder that contains a background image (you may be able to find some that were

included on your operating system). It can be a prefabricated background file, or another photograph that you've selected.

3. When the list of files displays on the Files list, click on Open. Your background image will appear in your file.

Adding the Final Touches

Congratulations! You've just completed your first online photo album. Once you've got your photographs and captions together, look everything over and add the final touches. Maybe you'd like to create a cover page to set off your best picture. Remember to vary your alignment to keep the individual pages interesting, and be sure the text is legible and appealing. Don't be afraid to get silly, but it's just as easy to strive for an elegant, clean design. Don't forget to share the album by sending it as an e-mail attachment or printing it out.

AOL's GraphicSuite

AOL offers a CD-ROM-based collection of tools for editing and organizing digital pictures. GraphicSuite (figure 3.4) contains top-rated programs and utilities from many leading software publishers. Aside from all the tools you need, the CD includes 10,000 royalty-free photos and images. For further information, use keyword **GraphicSuite**.

43

Other Brilliant Ideas

Now that you've got the basics down, you can create all kinds of keepsakes and mementos to keep or give as gifts. Here are some ideas to get you going:

• Make a baby album. Whether you're the lucky parent or you want to celebrate a friend's or relative's new arrival, no one ever has enough pictures of a new baby. Creating a baby album is fun and easy. Send it to parents, grandparents, friends, and coworkers. Print out a copy and present it as a scroll tied up with a pink or blue ribbon.

• Design custom greeting cards. Open a picture in the Picture Gallery's image editing window, turn it upside down by clicking on Flip Image

44

Vertically, then save the image. Open a new file, insert the picture, and save the file. Print out the picture and fold the page over for an instant greeting card. If the picture is positioned too close to the lower edge of the page, return to the greeting card file, place your cursor above the picture, and press the Enter key a couple of times.

- Create custom notepads. Even the person who has everything can always use some scratch paper for jotting down notes. Place a small digital picture (no more than two inches by two inches) in a new file, enter your witty caption below it in a fun or elegant font, and center the picture and the text. Print out 20 copies and staple them inside a manila folder (the staples should go along the top of the pages). Print out another copy and glue it to the front of the folder, as a cover page.

- Create calendars, screen savers, and more with software like Creative Wonders' PhotoCreations All-in-One Studio (visit Creative Wonders at keyword **Creative Wonders**). You can use just about any theme for calendar pictures, including pets, gardens, cars, friends, and family members. (Chapter 10 explains how to have calendars professionally printed.)

PHOTOGRAPHY POINTERS

Sooner or later, everyone grabs a camera and tries to take pictures of someone or something. No matter how much or how little experience you have, there are useful tips to remember and use. Here are a few you might find invaluable:

1. **Keep your camera ready.** You can't get that great shot if your camera is locked in the trunk of your car or at the bottom of your suitcase.

2. **Get close.** The closer you get to your subject, the better your pictures are going to be. Getting close eliminates unnecessary backgrounds and shows your subject more clearly.

3. **Keep people busy.** Keeping people busy while you're photographing them gives your pictures a sense of spontaneity and eliminates stiff or static poses: your subjects will have more natural and relaxed expressions.

4. **Use simple backgrounds.** Using simple backgrounds keeps the focus on your subject and gives you clearer, stronger compositions.

5. **Place your subject off center.** Putting your subject a little off center makes your composition more dynamic and interesting.

6. **Include foreground objects in scenic pictures.** When you put objects in the foreground of scenic pictures, you add a sense of distance, depth, and dimension.

7. **Hold your camera steady.** Clear, sharp pictures are impossible to get if you don't hold your camera steady, so press the shutter button gently, brace your arm, or use a tripod if necessary.

8. **Look for good lighting.** Lighting is the most essential component of taking good pictures. Good lighting exposes film properly and makes your pictures more interesting, colorful, and flattering to your subject.

9. **Use your flash.** The flash built into most cameras can improve your pictures by providing extra light when you need it.

10. **Choose the right film.** There are different film speeds for different conditions. For example, 100-speed film is best for pictures taken in bright sunlight, 200-speed film is better for slow- to moderate-speed action and variable lighting situations, and 400-speed film is better for extended flash range and fast-action outdoor shots.

Adapted from *KODAK: Top Ten Techniques,* © Eastman Kodak Company, 1994–1998. Kodak's Web site is at http://www.kodak.com.

Knowledge of basic photography terms can help you take better pictures and discuss your new hobby with other photographers.

- **Ambient light** The available light around your subject; light already existing in an indoor or outdoor setting.
- **Angle of view** The area you see through the lens, determined by the lens type you use.
- **Background** The scene appearing behind the subject.
- **Backlighting** The light coming from behind the subject; this can make the subject stand out darkly against the background, producing a silhouette.
- **Camera angles** The position of the camera relative to the subject; this can be used to create the effect of an unusual viewpoint.
- **Contrast** The range of difference between light and dark areas in a picture or negative.
- **Cropping** Printing only part of the picture, usually to create a more pleasing effect or composition.
- **Definition** The clarity of detail in a photograph.
- **Diffuse lighting** Low or moderate contrast in lighting, like an overcast day.
- **Double exposure** Two pictures taken on the same frame of film or two negatives printed to overlap on one piece of photographic paper.
- **Exposure** The amount of time that film or print paper is exposed to light.
- **Fill-in light** Additional light like flashes, lamps, or reflectors that reduce necessary exposure time.
- **Flash** A brief and intense burst of light from a flashbulb or electronic flash unit to enhance available light for a picture.
- **Flat lighting** Lighting that gives pictures very little contrast and a minimum of shadows.
- **Foreground** The area between the camera and the subject.
- **Front lighting** Light illuminating the side of the subject facing the camera.
- **Overexposure** Too much light reaching the film, producing a very light print.
- **Panorama** A broad view of a scene, usually a scenic picture.
- **Photo file index print** Small prints or thumbnail-sized versions of pictures that make ordering reprints and enlargements easier.
- **Processing** Developing, fixing, and washing exposed film or photographic paper to produce negatives or prints.
- **Side lighting** Light striking the subject to the side of the camera, producing high contrast shadows and highlights.
- **Soft lighting** Light producing low or moderate contrast, like on an overcast day.
- **Timed exposure** Long exposure made in seconds or minutes, usually with the aid of a tripod.
- **Underexposure** When too little light reaches the film and produces a dark or muddy print.

- Design coffee mugs and T-shirts. Put your mug on a mug! Use a group photo from a recent reunion or celebration, a picture of your dog or cat, your backyard, your trip to the Grand Canyon, your kids—anything you can think of. (Chapter 10 tells you how to use digital pictures to prepare customized gifts and have them printed for you.)

- Make your own reprints. Why pay to have reprints of your favorite photos made? With a color printer, you can create your own reprints anytime you want and give them away as gifts. (Chapter 13 tells you how to enlarge, reduce, touch up, and print your digital pictures.)

- Become your group's historian. If you've stayed in touch with old classmates, former coworkers, or any other special group of people over the years, make a "where are they now" photo album. Gather old and new photographs, along with information about everyone's current lives. For each person, put the photographs of their former and current selves together, along with a paragraph about what they were doing then, and what they're doing now. Share your efforts with the whole group.

- Create an electronic portfolio. If you're an artist, designer, or craftsperson, create an online photo album of your best work. Meet other artists and post your portfolio at the Computer Artists Online forum (keyword: **AOTW**).

- Show off your collections. No matter how obscure you think your collection is, you can pretty much bet that someone on the AOL service shares your interest. Get together with fellow collectors to exchange albums and tips. Start off with a visit to the Hobby Central forum (keyword: **Hobby**).

4

FAMILY TREES AND OTHER PERSONAL RECORDS

Running out of gift ideas for your family? A lively, illustrated family tree can provide years of enjoyment and bring you and the people you care about closer together. Imagine the dimensions digital imaging can add to the traditional paper chart of names and lines. It's easy and fun. This chapter will take you through the steps of creating a basic genealogical chart using your favorite family photographs. You'll also learn how to trace your roots with the Genealogy forum and how to take advantage of some great ways to create other kinds of personal records, including a home inventory, time capsule, address book, and recipe book.

You can start right now with a simple chart for your immediate family. Don't worry if you don't have all the facts about everyone, or all the photographs you want. You can always add more text and pictures later. A number of AOL and Internet Web sites can help you trace your ancestors, do research, and gather information. Some of these sites even provide access to experts who can help you with any hurdles you might encounter. Finally, ask your relatives plenty of questions. They'll relish the opportunity to dish out names, dates, and old family stories.

Getting Started

Begin by opening a blank document and typing a list of the people in your immediate family. This can include you, your partner, and your children, along with your and your partner's parents, brothers, and sisters. Then add some information about everyone on the list. When you're finished, save this document so you can copy the information into your family tree or other files as needed.

Now your family tree is starting to shape up. But who wants to look at all that text? Pictures will add tremendous visual appeal. If you don't have photographs of everyone, that's OK. Use pictures to represent that family member's preferences or traits. If you have a grandmother from Finland, include a beautiful picture of a fjord. If your uncle spends all his time in the garage with his woodworking hobby, find appropriate clip art to appear with his name. The Pictures area (keyword: **AOL Pictures**) on the Interests channel can get you started with ideas, resources, and images to use. You can also get help from the AOL Gallery (keyword: **Gallery**), where you'll see how fellow AOL members use images and find clip art and other resources.

Building a Family Tree

Once you've entered your information and gathered your pictures, you can begin building your family tree. It's so easy—you don't even need to go online. Before you get started, however, take a moment to think about how you want to lay out your family tree.

You can design the document however you like, but both amateur and professional genealogists generally use one of the following two formats:

- **Narrative format** tells a story about each person in your chart, like the example shown in figure 4.1. The narrative format gives you more flexibility for including detailed information and photographs for each person on your chart.

- **Linked format** shows how family members are related to each other, but only includes basic information about each person. This more traditional format looks like a pyramid or organizational flowchart, as shown in figure 4.2.

You can include the following facts about family members:

- Date of birth
- Place of birth
- Marital status and wedding date
- Children
- Occupations
- Places lived
- Date of death (where relevant)
- Nationality (where relevant or known)

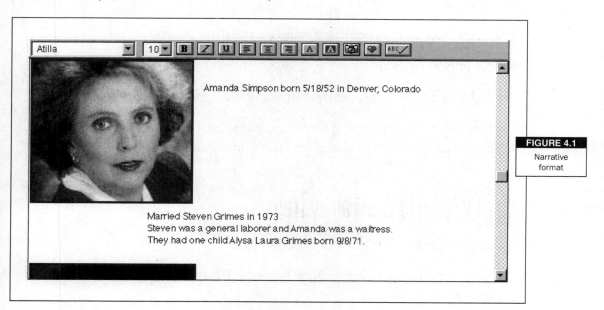

FIGURE 4.1
Narrative format

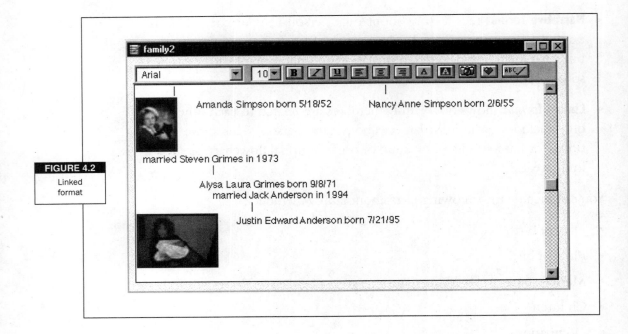

FIGURE 4.2

Linked format

Window contents:

family2

Arial | 10 | **B** *I* U

Amanda Simpson born 5/18/52   Nancy Anne Simpson born 2/6/55

married Steven Grimes in 1973

Alysa Laura Grimes born 9/8/71
married Jack Anderson in 1994

Justin Edward Anderson born 7/21/95

52

But these cold, hard facts say nothing about what your family members are like. Add color to your family tree by including everyone's:

- Educational achievements

- Military service record, branch of military, and dates of service

- Special honors or awards

- Date of first communion, bar mitzvah, or other significant religious data

- Favorite ice cream, singers, quotations, jokes, movies, family stories—whatever you can think of that gives insight into their personalities.

Adding Pictures to Your Family Tree

To create your family tree:

1. Open a new file by selecting New from the File menu. The blank editing window will open.

2. Open the Picture Gallery by selecting Open Picture Gallery from the File menu. When the Open Picture Gallery dialogue box appears, you can browse for the folder that contains the pictures you want to use.

3. To insert a picture, select an image from the Picture Gallery. Click on it and drag the picture into your document.

4. Select Save As from the File menu. When the Save As dialogue box appears, choose a name and click on Save.

5. Type the information for the person in the picture, as explained earlier in this chapter. If you have already created a document to store this information, you can copy and paste blocks of text next to the appropriate pictures.

6. Repeat steps 4 and 5 for each family member.

Congratulations! You've just created a family tree you can e-mail to everyone in it. You probably have cousins and other family members you've been out of touch with for years—or never even met. You can now meet or get reacquainted with this creative project. Print out copies for relatives who don't have e-mail. If you don't have a color printer, AOL offers a wide variety of graphics services or can guide you to a service bureau in your area.

Your family tree will get more complicated when you add more ancestors. But never fear, there are software packages that can help. You can purchase them through the AOL Store's Software Shop (keyword: **Software Shop**) under Home & Health. The Genealogy Forum (keyword: **Roots**) also guides you to other software programs and resources.

Tracing Your Ancestors through the Genealogy Forum

Your family tree can develop into a wonderful multigenerational project as you, your children, and your relatives continually update and expand it. The Genealogy Forum makes tracing your ancestors fun and educational. So prepare yourself and your family to embark on a long and fascinating journey. As a bonus, while researching your background, you may discover intriguing facts about the countries your ancestors called home, reconnect with long-lost relatives, and meet all kinds of people along the way.

To get started, enter the keyword **Roots**. The Genealogy Forum offers a vast selection of resources, including guides to AOL and Internet genealogy sites, a Genealogy Store, advice from experts, a chat room for exchanging information with other AOL members, software, and helpful research tools. You can search for names by region, ethnic group, and public records. Or use the File Library to research histories and cultures, review chat session logs, access related newsletters, and more.

Other Ideas for Creating Personal Records

Using the same basic approach as when making your family tree, you can let your mind wander and come up with all kinds of useful and fun things to do. Create a graphic record of personal property for insurance purposes. Set up an address book with pictures of everyone. Create an instant file for favorite recipes. Work on special projects with your children. Here's how.

Build a Home Inventory for Insurance Purposes

Although nobody likes to think about bad things happening to their homes or possessions, it's a smart idea to keep a collection of photographs in case you ever need to file an insurance claim. First, take pictures of any property you have insured. Take your roll of film to the lab, and have them make a photo CD and prints. Store the prints and negatives in a safe deposit box or other secure place.

Then:

1. Open a new file by selecting New from the File menu. Name the file.

2. Display the pictures from your photo CD in the Picture Gallery.

3. Drag the pictures into your document and enter the facts about each one: description, date purchased, purchase price, and any other pertinent details. Some items (such as antique jewelry) may require a professional appraisal.

4. Save your file and copy it onto two floppy disks. Keep one in a safe place and give the other one to your insurance agent.

Remember to update your file when you purchase new items or dispose of old ones. Your inventory won't do you much good if it's missing your new car that's just been stolen.

Make a Time Capsule

Create memories for the future with a time capsule. What an imaginative way to use the creative potential in your computer! While this project is ideal for families, organizations or groups of friends can try it too. First, gather together special stories, photographs, video and audio snippets of news broadcasts and television shows or favorite songs—anything you can think of that is currently of interest. Then pick a date in the future—maybe a milestone anniversary of some sort, a reunion, or a special birthday. When the date arrives, open the file and enjoy your memories.

Here's how to create a time capsule:

1. Create a new file for your time capsule, and name the file.

2. Open the Picture Gallery to move digital pictures into the file. For instructions on adding multimedia and special effects, see chapter 14.

3. Save the time capsule file and pick your future date. If it's too far in the future to mark in a datebook, use a personal information manager program to remind you as the big day approaches (AOL can help you find the right software).

4. When the time capsule date grows near, plan a special celebration. And make sure to take plenty of pictures so you can use them in future time capsules! (Go to keyword **Reminder** to set up a reminder to open them.)

Create an Address Book

Since becoming an AOL member, you've probably met people from all corners of the globe. And it's as easy to keep in touch with your new friends as it was to make them. A special Address Book, as shown in figure 4.3, can help you keep track of everyone. You can create a profile of all your friends, including how to contact them, their likes and dislikes, how you met them, and photographs. Access your Address Book anytime to get information or make updates—you don't need to go online. Simply click on Mail Center, then select Address Book from the drop-down menu.

Here's how to add a profile to your Address Book:

1. Open your Address Book and click on New Person.

2. In the New Person dialogue box, enter profile information—such as the person's name, e-mail address, and whatever notes you'll find useful—in the appropriate text fields.

3. To add a picture or photograph, select the Picture tab, then click on Select Picture to browse for the picture you want to use, as shown in figure 4.4.

You can also create mailing groups—lists of people you frequently send the same information to.

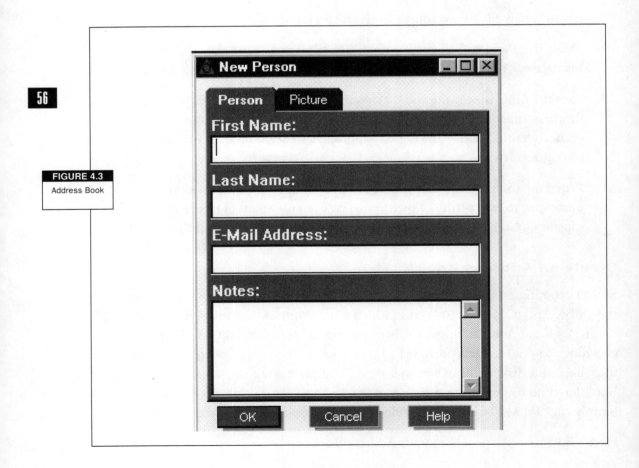

FIGURE 4.3
Address Book

Here's how to create a new mailing group:

1. Click on the New Group icon at the bottom of the Address Book window.

2. When the New Group dialogue box appears, enter a name for your group and a list of e-mail addresses in the appropriate text fields.

3. When you finish, click on OK to save the new group and return to the Address Book window.

To edit your contact information, click on the Edit icon at the bottom of the Address Book window and enter your changes when the appropriate dialogue box appears. You can also delete entries by selecting the ones you want deleted and clicking on the Delete icon at the bottom of the Address Book window.

Use your Address Book to send, copy, blind-copy, and forward messages to people. To address the current e-mail message, simply launch the Address Book, select a name, and click a message option. The Address Book automatically inserts the address in your message.

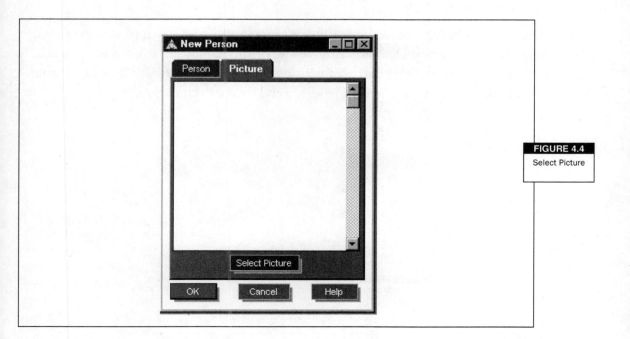

FIGURE 4.4
Select Picture

Cook Up an Online Recipe Book

Think of the special recipes you can be counted on to cook for friends and family. Or dishes you've always *wanted* to make, but when the mood hits, you're left scratching your head and saying, "Now where did I put that piece of paper with the recipe?" With an online recipe book, you'll never again have to deal with those loose pages torn from magazines or passed along by a friend. Use your imagination in making up the file—along with the recipe itself, include digital pictures of the prepared meal, a picture of the person who gave you the recipe, or a picture of you and your friends enjoying the finished product. Printed copies make wonderful gifts.

Here's how to create a recipe book:

1. Create a new file for your recipe book, and name the file.

2. Open the Picture Gallery to move digital pictures into your recipe book. If you don't have any appropriate pictures, download some clip art.

3. Type the text for your Chicken Surprise next to or below the picture.

4. Repeat steps 2 and 3 to add more recipes.

5. When you finish, save the file. Remember to update it whenever you have a new recipe.

The ideas in this chapter represent only a few samples of the rich resources at your fingertips. In the next chapter we move away from family and toward new friends. By learning how to create and post your own personal profile, you'll be better able to put yourself "out there"—for friendship and maybe even romance.

5

THE GREAT PHOTO SWAP: POSTING PICTURES FOR MATES, DATES, AND ONLINE BUDDIES

Think of your new skills with digital pictures as an engraved invitation to the biggest party on earth. In this chapter you'll learn ways to meet new friends and potential dates and share pictures with old friends and family. We'll take you through each step of posting your pictures plus an online bio in AOL picture areas, creating a personal profile you can e-mail to people, and setting up online events featuring digital pictures. So read on if you want to meet new people, see old friends, or look for romance. And who doesn't?

Here are just a few of the ways you can share your digital pictures:

- **Post them on AOL.** Whether you're looking for friendship or romance or simply want to let the world know who you are, AOL offers numerous areas where you can post your picture and some biographical information.

- **Create a personal profile.** You can also create a personal profile to e-mail to your online Buddies.

- **Visit online forums and chat areas.** Whenever you exchange information with people and talk with them regularly, you naturally get curious about what they look like. They want to see you too. Forums and chat areas allow you to exchange digital pictures of yourselves.

- **Have an online party.** Reserve a chat room and host a party—with pictures. First, send out some enticing invitations, then gather the pictures of everyone attending and e-mail them to all the guests. When guests arrive in the chat room, toast one another while you chat and enjoy the pictures together.

Create a Personal Profile

Your personal profile document, like the one shown in figure 5.1, is a useful tool to create so you don't have to keep introducing yourself to new online contacts. Think of it as a digital calling card, complete with a flattering photo. Send it to current and potential online pals as an e-mail attachment, and encourage them to send you theirs. Those who don't have one might be inspired by seeing yours.

Your personal profile does more than save you from having to type the same information every time you meet someone new. Since AOL posting areas only let you include a limited amount of biographical information, personal profiles give you a chance to get creative and let your personality shine through.

Creating a personal profile is easy. Select New from the File menu to open a blank document, click on the Picture icon (the camera) to insert your digital picture, and then type your information.

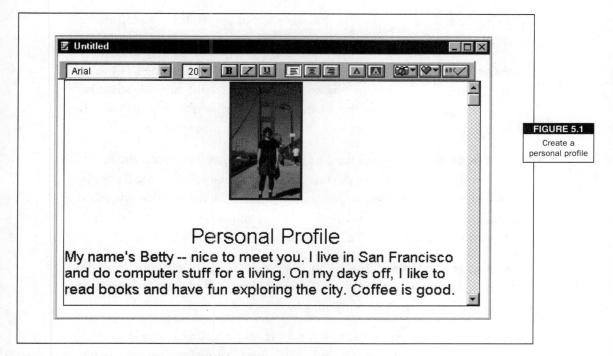

FIGURE 5.1

Create a
personal profile

Putting Your Best Foot Forward

First impressions count—even when you're online. Your personal profile can reveal as much or as little about you as you want. Be quirky, serious, hilarious, or intriguing, but always put your best foot forward. Don't worry about being perfect. Concern yourself with conveying a real sense of who you are to someone who knows nothing about you.

When creating your personal profile, consider the following:

- **Information to include.** You'll probably want to provide general information like your name, your age, where you live, what you do for a living, whether you're married or have kids. You can also tell people what you love to do in your spare time, what your favorite and least favorite things are, what pets you have, and so on. In figure 5.1, we can read only three lines about Betty, but those three lines together with her picture tell us a lot about her.

- **Information *not* to include.** Don't give out your street address and phone number (at least not until you get to know someone better). Many people choose not to reveal their real names, but go by their screen name instead.

- **Make your expectations clear.** Avoid needless misunderstandings. If you're only looking for friendship, say so: "I like basketball, Arnold Schwarzenegger, and Chihuahuas. I'd love to hear from you if you do too." If you're in the market for true love, wear your heart on your sleeve.

- **Use a few details.** You don't have to be a great writer to create a great personal profile. A key detail or two can help your personality come through. Explain that you saw *Sleepless in Seattle* nine times, that you've just taken up rock climbing, that your ideal Saturday morning is spent reading in bed with a big mug of coffee at your side.

- **Humor goes a long way.** Humor always breaks the ice, and your comedic style reveals a lot about the kind of person you are. Tell your favorite joke or repeat a funny story about yourself.

- **Keep it brief.** Sure, you want to tell people about yourself. But don't deluge them with information. You can reveal more as you get better acquainted. Limit your personal profile to a page or page and a half.

62

Posting Your Picture on AOL

Chat rooms and forums are two good places to meet people who share your interests and to share your personal profile. Or drop by the online dating and romance areas like Love@AOL (keyword: **Love@AOL**) for love, AOL style. You can also take a look at other AOL members' pictures and get to know them better. So log on and find that perfect pen pal or online flirtation ... or help them find you. But before you post your pictures, read the rules. Some AOL posting areas accept GIF, JPEG, BMP, TIF, and PICT files, but others accept only GIFs and JPEGs.

You can get started by visiting the following AOL areas:

- **AOL Portrait Gallery.** Enter the keyword **Gallery** to view photographs of your fellow AOL members or check out AOL's party pictures. Here you'll also find instructions for posting your own picture.

- **Family Gallery.** Enter the keyword **Family Gallery** to drop by and relax for a while. Hang out in the Rec Room, get to know AOL members and their families, and exchange digital pictures and slide shows. The Family Gallery also features a special Family Children's Album and a Special Events Gallery so you can share your celebrations.

- **Love@AOL.** Meet dates or future mates by entering the keyword **Love@AOL**. Here you can view people's picture bios and post your own. This area also gives you tips on how to create an appealing personal bio and guides you through the steps of posting it. Don't miss the Romance Connection (keyword: **Romance Connection**), a great place to post a personal ad.

- **Digital City Pen Pals.** If you're looking for a pen pal, visit the Digital City Pen Pals area, as shown in figure 5.2 (keyword: **Digital City Pen Pals**). Here you can search for potential pen pals by city or by interests, and post your picture with some biographical information. If you'd like to correspond with someone from a foreign country, enter the keywords **Special Delivery** to visit the International Pen Pals area. Choose a pal who's as near as your own city or as far as the farthest continent.

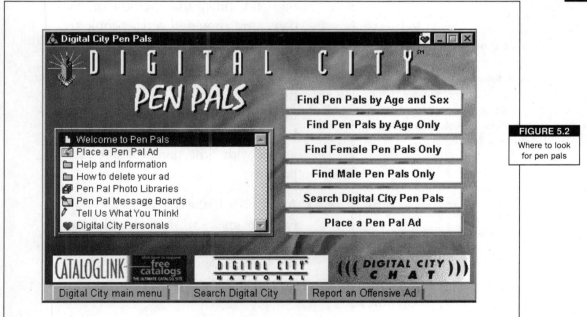

FIGURE 5.2

Where to look for pen pals

Picture files are lots of fun, but they're much larger than text files. That's why it takes longer to upload images to posting areas or send them via e-mail or Instant Message. You can get around this problem by compressing your files with a program called WinZip. Compressing your files makes them smaller so you can send them to people more quickly. When your recipients download the file, they can unzip it to restore it to its normal size, and view the picture. WinZip is easy to use, and most Windows users have it. The shareware program has a $29 registration fee and you can download it from the Software Center (keyword: **Software**). Click on Software Search, then on Shareware to find it. Keep in mind that AOL 4.0 will compress multiple files for you when you send e-mail.

Hosting Online Picture Parties

Everyone loves a good party. Why not have one online? All you have to do to host a picture party is reserve a chat room and encourage your guests to share their digital pictures. Although you can't actually display pictures in the chat room itself, you can gather the pictures and send them to everyone beforehand so you can all view them together. With a little creativity, planning, and organization, you and your family, friends, and online pals will have a fun new way to hang out together.

Steps for planning the perfect online picture party:

1. Pick an appropriate chat room to meet in.

2. Send attractive invitations to your guests. The invitations should include the date, time, and location of the party, and should also tell people to send you pictures by a certain date.

3. Gather the pictures together and send them to everyone a few days before the party. If your guests don't already know each other, prepare a list of names with little blurbs about each person.

4. Arrive early in the chat room and wait for your guests to show up. Play the talk show host—guide people through the pictures and keep the conversations going.

Think about how you want to present the collected photographs to your guests. You have a variety of options for assembling your pictures:

- **Zip them.** You can use WinZip to put your pictures in a compressed, self-extracting ZIP file. Send the ZIP file to your guests as an e-mail attachment, and provide instructions on how to extract the files to a special folder. During the party, everyone can view the pictures in the Picture Gallery. (For more about compression and ZIP files, see the "Compressing Files for Easy Transfer and Storage" sidebar in this chapter.)

- **Create a document.** You can include all of the pictures in a document and add a caption to each picture. This takes more time than simply zipping up the pictures and sending them, but provides more entertainment for your guests. (For more information about creating documents with digital pictures and captions, see chapter 4.)

PHOTOGRAPHY TERMS YOU SHOULD KNOW

Here are some more helpful photography terms. By the time you finish this book, you'll be talking like the pros:

- **B (Bulb) setting** Also referred to as the *shutter speed* setting, the bulb setting lets you keep the shutter open so you can take timed exposures.
- **Close-up** A picture with the main subject close to the lens.
- **Composition** The arrangement of elements in a picture, including the main subject, foreground, background, and supporting subjects.
- **Film speed** The sensitivity of film to light as indicated by a number; the higher the number (100, 200, 400), the more sensitive to light or faster the film.
- **Panning** Following a moving object with the camera to keep the object in the same relative position, or moving the camera across a stationary object to get a panoramic effect.
- **Range finder** Aids in focusing. Found on most cameras.
- **Simple camera** A camera that has few or no adjustments to make before taking a picture.
- **Aperture** The opening in the camera that lets light pass through to expose the film.
- **Pan or panochromatic film** A type of film that records all colors in tones of the same relative brightness as the human eye sees.

You can also use AOL's Personal Publisher—the Web page creation tool (keyword: **Personal Publisher**)—to set up an online picture party site. You don't have to know anything about Web pages. As long as your images are saved as GIF or JPEG files, the Personal Publisher can get you up and running in a snap. (Chapter 12 tells you about some programs you can use to convert your digital pictures to GIFs and JPEGs.) Once you create your page, arrange the pictures, and enter your text, the Personal Publisher helps you upload all the files to your AOL Web site. When your guests arrive at the party, give them your URL, tell them to launch their browsers, and view the pictures together. (For more about creating Web pages, see chapter 7.)

Online Party Ideas

Now that you know how to throw an online picture party, it's time to think of a theme. Let your imagination run wild, and send out festive invitations and announcements, like the one shown in figure 5.3.

Here are a few ideas to get you warmed up:

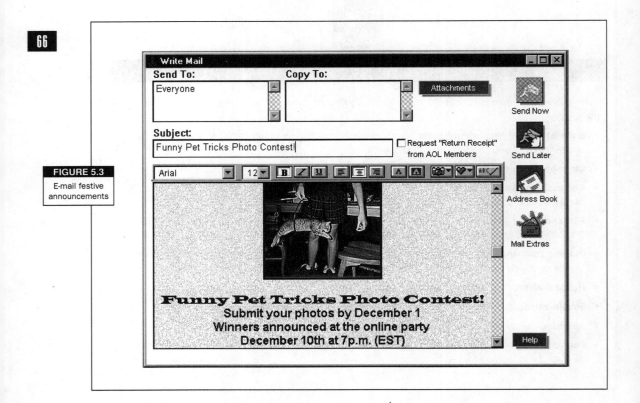

FIGURE 5.3
E-mail festive announcements

- **A contest.** What about a digital pictures contest for the people in your favorite forum or chat room? Do you and your online pals frequent the Hobbies area? Host a Crazy Crafts contest and encourage people to send pictures of their wackiest creations. Is gardening the preferred topic? Host a Beautiful Garden contest. Whatever interests you and your friends, you can build a contest around it. Choose three or four people as judges, and e-mail elegant awards certificates to the winner and runners-up. Announce the winners at the online picture party, or post the winning photos on your Web page.

- **A day-in-the-life slide show party.** You don't have to wait for a special occasion to host a digital picture party. You and your online pals can get to know each other better by creating and sharing slide shows about your daily lives. Take pictures of typical daily scenes, like the old clunker that takes a half hour to start on cold mornings, the crowded train you take to work, your neighborhood park, and the place where you pick up your morning coffee. You can also highlight interests and recent accomplishments—like the picture of you running in that marathon to benefit your favorite charity. Show your pals a picture of you relaxing in your favorite room in your apartment or house. After the party, you'll find yourself thinking things like,

INDEXING AND ARCHIVING YOUR PICTURES ONLINE

The AOL service has many areas where you can upload or store your digital pictures. All of these areas have some basic rules for archival and storage:

1. The digital size of the file should not exceed 2.5 megabytes (MB), but it is preferable to use a file of less than 1 megabyte in size.

2. The digital picture should be 125 by 125 pixels in overall viewing size. You can crop and resize pictures to fit those specifications.

3. The digital picture should be in one of these formats: GIF, JPEG, or JPG. However, some areas do let you upload BMP, PIC, or TIF file formats. Check the guidelines for the area before you upload a digital picture.

4. You should name your digital file using your screen name or the first eight characters of your screen name.

5. The digital photos you want to upload should adhere to the AOL Terms of Service agreement (keyword: **TOS**).

6. Many of these areas require you to be 18 or older to upload or post your digital picture. Young people can post pictures to designated areas on Kids Only (keyword: **Kids Only**) and other children's areas.

"Gee, Suzy didn't seem like the dirt-biking type … and I had no idea that Fred plays jazz guitar."

- **A costume party.** Why does Halloween have to last only one day? Get people together anytime the mood strikes for an online costume party and have them send pictures. You and your guests can hang out in the chat room and talk about how you thought up your costumes and what you did on Halloween. Vote on the best costume and e-mail prize certificates to the winners.

- **An online family reunion.** Everybody's busy. And many family members live hundreds or thousands of miles apart. If you haven't talked with Aunt Millie and her crew in ages, it may be time to host an online family reunion. In your invitation ask everyone to send recent pictures of themselves and scenes from their lives. Gather the pictures into a digital photo album and e-mail copies to everyone, or post the pictures on your Web page. When the party begins, catch up on each other's lives—and stop feeling guilty that you haven't visited or written.

You and the people you meet online can cement new relationships and rebuild old ones through digital picture parties. Now that you know how to host one, what are you waiting for?

6

CELEBRATING! INVITATIONS, NNOUNCEMENTS, ND OTHER WAYS TO SPREAD GOOD NEWS

Your daughter just got married. Your friends are the proud parents of a new baby girl or boy. You've finally gotten that big promotion. Share the good news!

In the old days, people shouted good news from the rooftops. With digital pictures and America Online, you can save your vocal cords and reach a lot more people. This chapter introduces you to a few ways you can use technology to dazzle your friends and family while celebrating special occasions. If you're feeling ambitious, you can even pep up your online communications with a little multimedia.

Getting the Word Out

Anyone can send people store-bought invitations and announcements through the mail. But you've got a much bigger range of creative expression with online communications. Plus, you can spread the news to more people in a shorter amount of time. And, thanks to e-mail, you can send digital pictures to as many people as you want. Of course you'll get around to making copies of your photos for family and close friends. But printing and snail-mailing 30 or so pictures to friends and relatives can be expensive.

Here are a few hot ideas for designing attractive, personalized invitations, announcements, greeting cards, and more:

- **Embed digital pictures in an e-mail message.** E-mail offers you the fastest way to design an invitation or announcement with a digital picture and send it off. You can embed your digital picture directly in the e-mail message, as shown in figure 6.1, add a festive background image or color, and use the editing tools to jazz up your fonts.

- **Include digital pictures with file attachments.** If you have another program you enjoy using to create special files, attach it to the e-mail message. But make sure the application allows you to save to a file format people can open even if they don't have that particular application. You can also use special imaging software to convert and touch up files, as explained in chapter 11.

- **Write text directly on the image itself and attach it to your e-mail message.** If your digital picture is formatted as a BMP file, you can open it in Windows 95's Paint program and add text directly to the picture, as shown in figure 6.2.

- **Create your message in a word processing program.** Today's word processing applications offer a variety of formatting options that no e-mail program can match. You can design and lay out your personalized message and save it as an RTF (Rich Text Format) file. This ensures that just about anyone can open and save it, regardless of the word processing program they use.

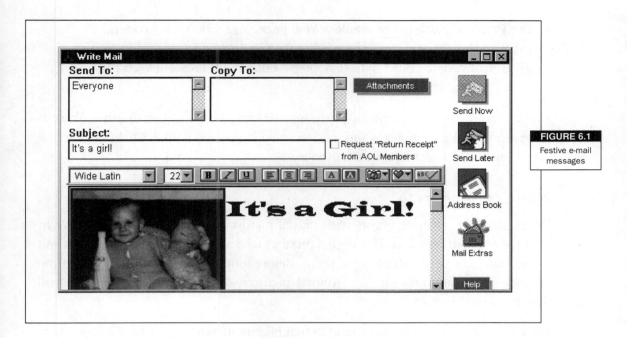

FIGURE 6.1
Festive e-mail messages

FIGURE 6.2
Windows 95's
Paint program

- **Use Personal Publisher to create a Web page.** You won't have to send e-mail attachments or worry about whether people can view your file. Simply e-mail people your URL. (Chapter 7 talks about creating Web pages with Personal Publisher.)

And if you enjoy writing a good, old-fashioned letter, keep right on doing it. You can print out your digital pictures and send them with a personal note. Or, better yet, use digital pictures to create unique stationery.

When to Celebrate

When can you celebrate events with digital pictures? Anytime! You don't have to wait for a special occasion. Use digital pictures to design personalized greetings and let people know you're thinking of them. Before long, you'll find yourself inventing excuses for communicating with digital pictures. Your friends and relatives will delight in your new hobby.

Here are a few great reasons to send digital picture messages:

- **A new baby.** Has a friend, relative, or office mate recently welcomed a new addition to the family? Give the proud parents a wonderful gift: one less errand to run. Tell them you'd be happy to create and send announcements to everyone on their list. Have a digital picture made of the baby, and get to work!

- **Just thinking of you.** Send a greeting with a digital picture to someone you haven't talked with in a while. You can send her a photograph of yourself or of the two of you together. Or download and include a digital picture, video, or sound file that reminds you of her or that would remind her of you—for example, a scene from a place you've visited together or a sound clip from a song you both love.

- **Weddings.** Take plenty of pictures at the next wedding you attend and send them with messages to the happy couple and guests online. If the wedding is your own, send announcements to colleagues, classmates, and acquaintances who couldn't make the big day.

- **Office parties.** Your department raced through the big deadline with flying colors. Your company is launching the greatest product ever. Or maybe you've just relocated to a new office or have a holiday party coming up. Celebrating milestones and big occasions with coworkers, clients, and partners builds a sense of teamwork while rewarding accomplishments. Take group pictures, before-and-after pictures of a work area, or a party in progress.

- **Birthdays and anniversaries.** Surprise your friends, business associates, spouse, boyfriend or girlfriend, mom, dad, Aunt Louise, and Uncle Harold by remembering birthdays and anniversaries with digital picture greetings and multimedia. Impress everyone with your foolproof memory—they don't have to know about your AOL Address Book with all the pictures and notes.

- **A new purchase.** Someone just bought a new condo? Your teenager just bought his first wreck with the money he's been saving up for years? Important purchases represent milestones in our lives. Take a picture and announce the good news or send your congratulations.

Tips for E-mailing Messages

E-mail is convenient, useful, and fun. But sending fancy messages with backgrounds and embedded images or attaching files takes a little practice. File attachments with digital pictures, sounds, or video can be surprisingly large. So before sending that QuickTime movie clip of a scene from Sharon Stone's latest movie to your friend (who is madly in love with her), make sure he has QuickTime software and doesn't mind receiving e-mail messages with large attached files. Multimedia, or files with lots of digital pictures, can easily tip the scales at an enormous 2MB—which can take a half hour to receive over the average user's 28 Kbps modem.

These guidelines can help you follow proper e-mail etiquette:

- **Send formatted e-mails with caution.** Some people aren't lucky enough to have exciting e-mail programs like yours. Before sending e-mails with formatted text or backgrounds, check with your recipient to see if it's OK. You can safely e-mail richly formatted messages to other AOL users and people who use Internet Explorer's or Netscape Communicator's e-mail program. Anyone else may have trouble with your messages—or won't see them as you intended.

You don't have to take photography courses to take good pictures of your family and friends. The following pointers can help you get comfortable behind a camera.

- Always have your camera ready—sometimes the best pictures happen by chance.

- Keep your camera lens clean to ensure sharp, clear pictures.

- Use the lens adjustments to bring your picture into sharper focus.

74

- **Use common fonts along with common sense.** Fancy fonts may tempt you, but try to resist. If the people you send messages to don't have the same fonts, your messages and file attachments won't display as you intend. Stick with fonts that everyone is likely to have: Times, Arial, Zapf Dingbats, Courier, and Wing Dings.

- **Avoid sending files larger than 250 KB.** Anything larger can take a long time for your correspondents to download. And don't forget that during all that time they won't be able to get any of their other e-mail. You can use a compression utility like WinZip to make your file smaller. (For more about compression, see chapter 5.)

- **Consider cross-platform compatibility issues.** If someone on your e-mail list just *loves* her Macintosh and would never part with it, think before attaching files. Macintosh users cannot open ZIP files unless they have a special program. You can send them to the AOL Software Center (keyword: **Software**) to see what is available. Also mention TUCOWS (http://www.tucows.com) where they can download UnZip for Macintosh. In addition, unless your Macintosh pal is a fellow AOL member, she needs special plug-ins to view PCX, BMP, and TIF images, as well as WAV and MIDI sound files, and AVI movies.

When you send e-mail, digital pictures, and attached multimedia files to other AOL members, you don't have to worry most of the time. AOL supports most common image and multimedia file formats to make your online experience seamless. But be kind to your pals who are not on the AOL service. Better yet, encourage them to get with the program and become members. If you're successful, you can earn a bonus; visit keyword **Friend** for details.

Adding Some Multimedia

There's no better way to liven up your invitations and announcements than with multimedia effects. AOL has built-in support for popular multimedia file formats for a richer online experience. Imagine sending invitations to a surprise party for your parents' golden anniversary with a button people can click on to play your parents' wedding song. Or sending a friend a digital birthday card with a video clip of his favorite movie star or musician, or a scene from the old neighborhood.

Working with multimedia is easy. First get the files—download them from AOL or record them yourself. Then design your personalized messages with a multimedia-capable software program such as Creative Wonders Greeting Card Maker. For details about this and other good programs, visit the Family Computing Center (keyword: **Family Computing**). Various channels and forums offer lots of downloadable audio, video, and digital picture files you can use to create impressive invitations, announcements, and greetings. Drop by American Greetings (keyword: **American Greetings**) to visit their electronic card collection and to purchase animated greeting cards. Or visit the PC Animation & Video Forum (keyword: **A&V Forum**) for software

MORE PHOTOGRAPHY TERMS YOU SHOULD KNOW

Following are more photography terms you will find useful:

- **Bracketing** Taking additional pictures of the same subject using longer and shorter exposures to compensate for uncertain light conditions.

- **Contact print** A print of the entire negative strip made by laying it directly on the photographic paper.

- **Candid pictures** Unposed portraits (often taken without the subject's knowledge).

- **Negative** Developed film. Negatives show the images in reverse.

- **Positive** A print from the negative or a slide transparency.

- **Print** A positive on photographic paper.

- **Thin negative** An underexposed or underdeveloped negative.

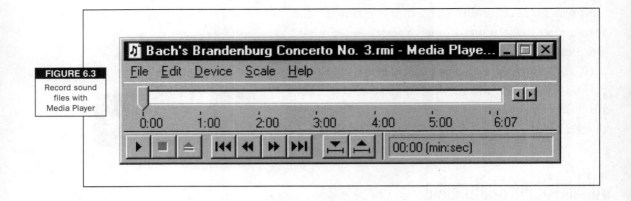

FIGURE 6.3
Record sound
files with
Media Player

resources, downloadable files, and more. Finally, try the Online Classroom area
(keyword: **Online Classroom**).

Getting Multimedia Files

So where do you get multimedia files, you ask? AOL and the Internet abound with
them. The channels and forums offer audio, video, and shockwave movie files that
you can download and use in your personalized messages. Shockwave movies are
fun-and-games animations that multimedia designers create in a program called
Macromedia Director. With minimal equipment and some creativity, you can also
make your own multimedia files. Windows 95's Media Player application, as shown
in figure 6.3, plays back sound files and AVI movies, and also records sound. AVI is
the standard video format for Windows. If you have a sound-capable system, all you
need to buy is a microphone in order to record audio. Recording video is more
expensive, but still within reach. Connectix's QuickCam and other similar products
start at around $100. They plug into the parallel port on your computer so you can
record AVI movies instantly. To find out more about QuickCam and similar products, visit the Digital Shop at keyword **Digital Shop**.

Here are some tips for personalizing your downloaded multimedia files:

- **Local scenes.** Just moved to Seattle? Visit Digital City (keyword: **Digital
  City**), download the sights and sounds of your new hometown, and send
  them to the folks back in San Diego.

- **The world of sports.** So, your office mate is an avid Boston Red Sox fan? Go to the Sports channel (keyword: **Sports**), get video highlights and pictures from a recent game, and send them to him.

- **Pop culture and entertainment.** Stop by the Entertainment channel (keyword: **Entertainment**) for clips from popular movies, television shows, and tunes. Send all your friends the best jokes from the latest episodes of *Seinfeld* and *Letterman*.

- **Online vacation.** Not enough time and money for two weeks in Barbados? Exchange pictures and videos of the glorious beaches you wish you'd visited, courtesy of the Travel channel (keyword: **Travel**).

No matter what subject grabs your interest, you can find the right sound, video, and digital picture files of it. AOL is overflowing with sites that offer sound effects, songs, television theme music, and video clips. Browse around and find the ones you want.

Communicating with Multimedia

You can easily share multimedia files by attaching them to e-mail messages. But don't stop there. You might not be able to embed movies and sounds directly in an

Just Married

photograph by Carol Grace
Just Married!

FIGURE 6.4
Create Web pages with sound and video

e-mail message (at least not *yet*), but a variety of inexpensive, user-friendly technologies can help you create exciting multimedia files that you can send as attachments.

Here's a list:

- **Personal Publisher.** The Web gives you an ideal medium for announcing good news with digital pictures and multimedia, as shown in figure 6.4. With AOL Personal Publisher, you can easily personalize a Web page with background music, embedded sound and video files, pictures, and more. You can either send an e-mail message with your URL, or attach all of your Web page files to the e-mail message so people can view your Web page offline. When you send people your Web pages or refer them to your Web site, you don't have to worry about what kind of computers or online service they use.

- **Presentation software.** Popular presentation programs like Microsoft PowerPoint and Gold Disk Astound make it simple to create slide shows and save the files so others can view them. When you use these programs, you don't have to worry about what fonts people have on their system.

- **Word processing software.** Some word processing programs, like Microsoft Word, offer multimedia features so you can insert videos and sound files into your documents. However, your recipient would have to have the same program—or a program with equivalent multimedia capabilities—in order to open your files.

In addition, a host of shareware and commercial software developers have created inexpensive, user-friendly multimedia programs including Slimshow, a shareware presentation program, and FunE-Cards, a shareware multimedia greeting card program. These programs are made especially for people who want to communicate with multimedia without having to spend a lot of money or delve into complex technologies. Search for retail software and shareware at the AOL Store and the Software Center.

7
CREATING WEB PAGES WITH PERSONAL PUBLISHER

Have you been admiring other people's Web pages and wishing you could create your own? Well, now's the time. Make up a Web page to share your photographs of the tucked-away village you visited in Italy (and that wonderful restaurant you discovered), the vase you made in your pottery class, your favorite neighborhood hangout, or your dog rough housing with his fellow canines in the park. Or build a community. For example, if you're an expert in calligraphy or model trains, you can attract fellow hobbyists to your page with news, tips, links to resources, and pictures of your own work.

Everyone can view Web pages no matter what kind of computer or browser they use. You can either add Web pages to your Web site, or you can send them as e-mail attachments so the recipient can view them in her Web browser.

Here are a few ideas to get you started:

- **Family album.** Create a family album (as explained in chapter 3) with digital pictures, then send the URL to all your relatives.

- **Hobby/special interest page.** Have fun promoting your interests. Fascinate others by displaying your collection of antique inkwells or your original artwork.

- **Business page.** Tell the world about the miniature toy soldiers you produce or the chimney sweep service you provide. (For more information, see chapter 9.)

- **Art page.** Here's your chance to publish the poetry you've been hiding in your desk drawer. Have an artist friend take photographs or draw pictures to accompany it. Or display your own paintings, crafts, or photographs.

- **My town.** Do you love the city you've just moved to? Have you lived all your life in the Southwest? Tell people all about it: display pictures and helpful links for those who might want to visit.

- **Online newsletter.** Use the Web to publish a full-color newsletter about anything that grabs you: polar bears, the rain forest, your home office, whatever. No printing costs!

- **Places I've been.** Are you a world traveler? Show people pictures of your adventures in the Australian outback, and share your perspectives on places most people only read about.

Jazz up your pages with sound, GIF animations, and scrolling marquees. This chapter guides you through the steps of creating your own Web site with Personal Publisher. It also gives you pointers on where to go for extra help, ideas, and resources for creating Web pages.

Personal Publisher makes Web publishing easy. However, before you begin authoring Web pages, it helps to know some of the basic terminology. Note that all pages on the WWW are created by using a special formatting language called HyperText Markup Language or HTML. An HTML document is a text file with HTML "tags" that tell browsers how to display and load text, images, links, and other page elements. Personal Publisher puts these tags in for you so you don't have to think about them. However, if you want more control over designing your pages and want to add advanced features, you'll need to learn more about HTML. It's easy once you get the hang of it and, as always, helpful resources abound (don't forget to check the Book Shop at the AOL Store).

- **HTML** HyperText Markup Language, the set of codes used to format Web pages.
- **Web browser** A program that displays Web pages.
- **HTML documents** These contain text and HTML codes. They are saved with the HTML or HTM file-name extension.
- **Associated files** Digital pictures, multimedia, and other files appearing on or launched from your Web pages.
- **Tags** HTML codes that tell the browser how to display text formatting, images, and other Web page elements.
- **Source code** The HTML text file within the HTML tags. Just as a set of gears, levers, wires, and a guy from Omaha, Nebraska, powered the Wizard of Oz, source code lies behind Web pages!
- **URL** Uniform Resource Locator, your Web page address (such as http://members.aol.com/mypage/index.html).
- **Links address** Images and text that jump you to another Web page or launch a multimedia file when you click on them; linked text is usually underlined.
- **Upload** Copying files from your computer to a directory on a server.
- **Download** Copying files from a server to your computer.
- **Personal Web space** A directory on AOL's server reserved for storing your Web pages.

81

Personal Publisher and Creating Web Pages

Web page publishing is complicated and technical, right? Wrong. In fact, if you know what you want to say and have all your files organized, putting together your

Web page can only take a minute—literally. Personal Publisher even allows you to create your Web pages offline. However, you do have to log on to the AOL service to put your Web page online where everyone can see it. The files will be stored on the AOL file server, which is automatically accessed by anyone who types your Web site address from the Net. Find out more about Web pages by visiting On the Net (keyword: **On the Net**).

Step by step, let's create a Web page about your trip to Australia right now. Note that the order of the steps may differ depending on the template chosen. The basic function will remain the same.

Step 1: Gather Your Material

Like anything else, once you get organized, you're halfway there. Before you begin, gather together all the materials you plan to use: photographs of Sydney, videos of kangaroos and koalas, clips from *Crocodile Dundee*. Think about what you want to say and what sites you want to create links to. Gather your digital pictures and multimedia files and place them in the same folder for easy access.

Here's what you'll need to do before you begin creating your Web page:

- **Create a Web page folder and move your files into it.** For your Web page to work properly, you should store everything that you plan to use in the same folder. This includes your digital pictures, Web pages (HTML documents), and multimedia files. Fortunately, Personal Publisher handles this task automatically as you use the Web page templates.

- **Convert your digital pictures to GIFs and JPEGs.** Web browsers can only display GIF and JPEG digital pictures, so you'll need to convert your TIF and PCX images. Personal Publisher will automatically convert your BMP files to JPEG. GIFs and JPEGs have small file sizes, which helps you make the most of the 2 MB of free Web space that AOL provides to every member. (Chapter 11 tells you more about graphics programs you can use to convert digital pictures.)

- **Compose your text.** Use the built-in text editor to write what you want to say on your Web page. Keep this file open while you create your Web page so you can copy and paste the text.

TIPS FOR DESIGNING YOUR WEB PAGE

Personal Publisher makes it quick and easy for you to create exactly the Web page you want. Here are a few tips for making the process even easier.

1. Be prepared. Make sure you have all the digital image, sound, video, animated pictures, and multimedia files you want to use and that you know where those files are stored on your computer.

2. Study other Web pages to get ideas for creating your own. To make yours appealing and informative, learn from what others have done.

3. Plan your Web pages in advance. Outline how you want your page to look, where you want graphics placed, and so on.

4. Test all your files to make sure they're functioning properly.

5. Test all sites you want to link; make sure the URLs all work and the pages haven't moved or disappeared.

6. Make sure your graphic files are as small as they can be without compromising their quality. Graphic files that are large take a long time to load. If they take too long, they can discourage visitors from remaining at your page.

7. Use all the resources on the AOL service to learn how to incorporate graphics and multimedia files on your Web page. The more you know, the better you will be at creating your Web page.

8. Check all the areas of your pages to make sure they look the way you want them to. Double-check all your links to make sure they all work properly once you put them on your Web page.

83

• **Gather your links.** Make sure all the pages you want to link to appear on your Favorites list. Personal Publisher displays a list of your Favorites to help you add links to your page. You can also type in the addresses using the Links option.

Don't worry if you haven't searched for the best movie clips yet, or if that last roll of film is still in your camera. You can update your page as often as you want. You can even create more than one page and link them together.

Step 2: Create Your Web Page

Next, select a design that best suits your needs from the list of templates. Then title your page—"Highlights from Down Under"—and pick a background and text colors to create the look you want. Once you've set up your page, you can enter or copy and paste your descriptions of everything you saw and did in Australia. To add links and create a custom color scheme, turn on Advanced Options. You can do this at any time by clicking on Advanced in the Personal Publisher application window. Keep in mind that each template offers slightly different options. These instructions apply to most of them.

To begin creating your Web page:

1. Use keyword **Personal Publisher**.

2. Click the Create button

3. When the Welcome to Personal Publisher dialogue box appears, as shown in figure 7.1, select a template from the scrolling list and click on Begin. Click on Preview Template to check it out before you make a commitment.

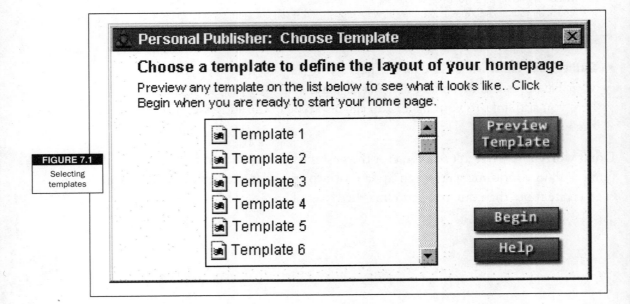

FIGURE 7.1

Selecting templates

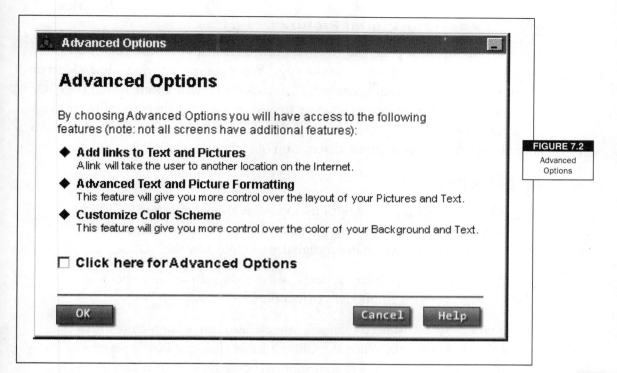

FIGURE 7.2
Advanced
Options

85

4. Select Advanced options, as shown in figure 7.2, if you'd like to make links, format text and pictures, and create your own page color scheme. (Otherwise, you'll remain in "basic" mode.)

5. When the Personal Publisher title window appears, type **Highlights from Down Under** in the text field, then click on Next.

6. When the background style and text color options appear, create a color scheme for your Web page. You can choose a color or image for your background, and also for your text, links, and visited links (links change color after the user clicks on them). When you finish, click on Next.

7. When the text dialogue box appears, enter your text, or copy and paste text from an open file. Text should be no more than a paragraph or two long. You can also add font and text styles to your page as you do when composing e-mail messages or documents in the text editor. When you finish entering and formatting your text, click on Next.

Step 3: Add Your Digital Pictures

Once you set up your page and add your text, Personal Publisher tells you exactly how to insert digital pictures into your page. You can use a drawing—like a logo or a cartoon—or a photograph that users can click on to visit another Web page. Or turn your digital picture into an image map: visitors can click on parts of image maps to jump to other locations. For example, clicking on your picture of a kangaroo could bring them to your funny description of seeing one for the first time.

To add a digital picture:

1. When the digital picture options appear, as shown in figure 7.3, click on Get My Picture to insert digital art from your own collection. Or click on Get Clip Art to insert digital art supplied by the AOL service.

2. When the Picture Gallery appears, select a digital picture to place on the page from the thumbnails that appear.

3. If you choose Advanced Options, you can also turn your picture into a link. Click on Link. When the Choose Links dialogue box appears, as shown in figure 7.4, select an option and click on OK. You can opt to link the entire picture, or create an image map by linking sections of the picture.

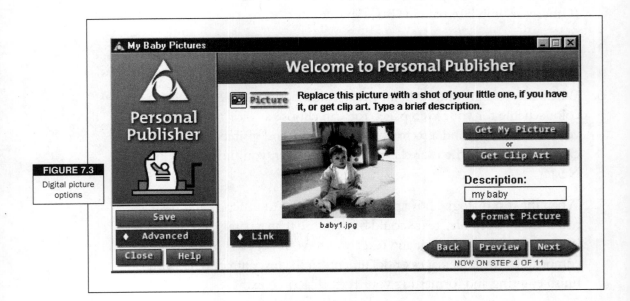

FIGURE 7.3

Digital picture options

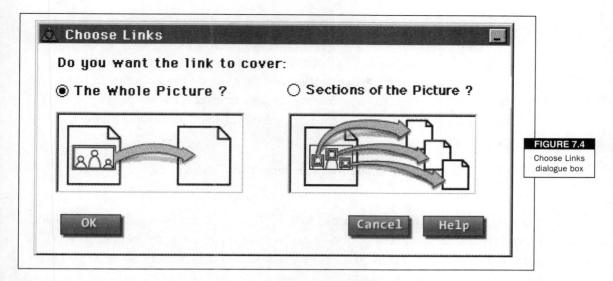

FIGURE 7.4

Choose Links
dialogue box

4. If you choose to link the entire picture, you will be asked to select a destination address from a number of options. You can also type an address. If you choose to create an image map, Personal Publisher helps you draw boxes around the sections you want to link, name the sections, and enter the address the link will take you to. Don't worry, the selection boxes you create won't appear in the image file or on the Web page.

87

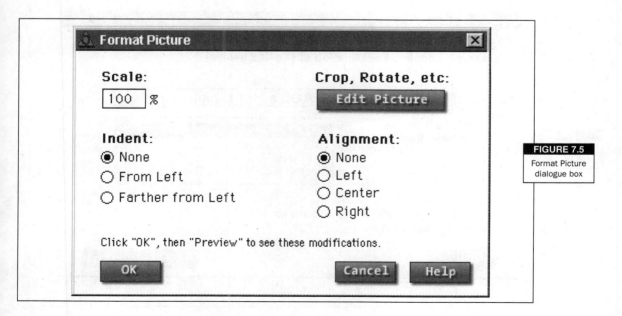

FIGURE 7.5

Format Picture
dialogue box

5. Edit your digital pictures and position them on the page by clicking on Format. When the Format Picture dialogue box appears, as shown in figure 7.5, opt to resize your picture (by entering a percentage in the Scale text field), edit your picture (by clicking on Edit Picture), or reposition the picture (by selecting options from the Indent or Alignment buttons). When you are finished editing and positioning your picture, click on OK.

6. Give your picture a name (use the default that's given, or assign your own name).

Do you like the way your pictures look? If so, several templates allow you to add more text and create links by clicking on Next to move on to the next step. You can click on Preview at any time to see how your Web page is coming along. If you need to make changes, click on Back.

Step 4: Make Links

You probably have some favorite links you want to include. If you're in advanced mode, a "links button" may appear that allows you to create a hyperlink from text or

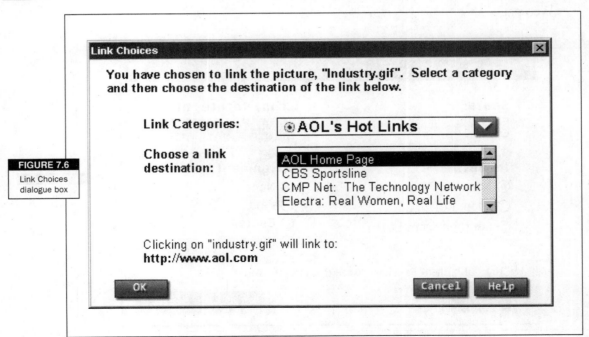

FIGURE 7.6

Link Choices dialogue box

pictures to another site. These links can jump visitors to your friends' pages, favorite Web sites, or resources on a topic of interest. Creating links is as easy as selecting text or a picture; just click on Add Link and select options from the Link Choices dialogue box (shown in figure 7.6). When you select a link category from the drop-down list, a list of link locations appears below. Hot Spots are AOL-recommended links. My Other Places are links to pages on your own Web site. The Within This Page option helps you create several links to different places on the same Web page. When you select a type of link, a list of your Favorites or available Web pages on your site displays. You can also link to places and files that don't appear on any of the lists by selecting the Type a URL option and entering a URL or filename manually.

To make links:

1. Select text or a picture, then click on the Add button.

2. When the Link Choices dialogue box appears, as shown in figure 7.6, choose the type of link you want to create from the Select a link category: pull-down list, then select a page from the list below.

3. Click on OK.

4. Repeat steps 1 to 3 until you've added all your links.

5. To remove a link, select the linked item and click on Delete.

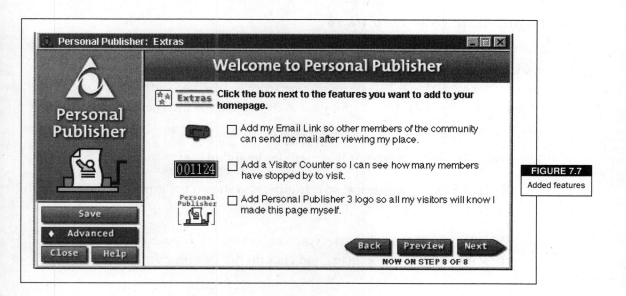

FIGURE 7.7
Added features

Step 5: Add Features

Now you're almost finished. Personal Publisher's final screen displays a list of features you can add to your Web page. You can make a link to your e-mail address, add a counter that keeps track of the number of visitors to your Web page, or add a logo telling everyone you created your page with Personal Publisher. To select options, click on the appropriate check box. Figure 7.7 shows you the added features you can include on your Web page.

- **E-mail Link.** When you click on the box to add your e-mail link, visitors to your page can e-mail you straight from your Web page. When they click on your link, a message composition window appears with your address entered so they can write a message and send it to you.

- **Visitor Counter.** By checking the Add Visitor Counter check box, you can show off how many people have visited your site. Personal Publisher adds a digital counter that displays on your Web page.

When you're finished selecting options, click on Done. Personal Publisher then asks you to save the file and give it a filename. Name your file (the default is "index.html") and save it to your Web folder containing your images and other files. (Hint: If you have several pages, you will want to be more descriptive. But make sure you finish with ".html".) Now you can upload your Web page and associated files to the AOL server.

Publishing Your Web Page

You've designed your Web page, checked it twice, and made it perfect. It's time to upload it to the World Wide Web. Personal Publisher makes it easy for you. AOL has reserved 10 megabytes of Web site storage space for each account (2 megabytes per screen name). Use this space to put your Web page on the Internet, or offer files others can download.

To upload a Web page to the AOL server, do the following:

1. When the Congratulations! screen appears as shown in figure 7.8, click on Publish.

2. When Personal Publisher asks you to give your Web page a filename, enter the same filename again, and click on the Publish button.

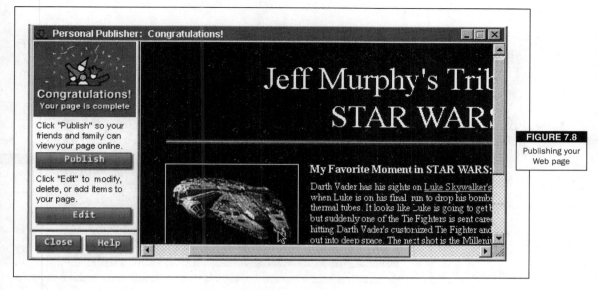

FIGURE 7.8

Publishing your
Web page

Your Web page is then stored on AOL's server. To get to it, use keyword **My Place.** Your Web address will be: http://members.aol.com/yourscreenname/index.html.

Editing Your Web Page

You can edit any item on your Web page by clicking on the Edit Item button (see figure 7.9). But suppose your already-published Web page announces a new arrival to your family…who is now almost a year old. Or everyone loves your festive New Year's page, but as July approaches it begins to seem a bit peculiar. Personal Publisher's site management features make managing your Web site easy. You can add and remove pages from the AOL server, preview unpublished pages, and link pages together. To begin managing your pages, open Personal Publisher and click on the Manage Your Pages button. When the page management options appear, as shown in figure 7.10, you can select options.

The window displays two lists. One list shows the pages you have published on AOL, and the other list shows unpublished files on your computer. You can choose what kind of files to display (such as HTML documents or images) by selecting an option from the Show drop-down list.

Here's everything you can do using Personal Publisher's site management features:

- **Publish and remove pages.** To publish a page from your computer to the AOL server, select a page from the Unpublished Pages on the Your Computer list and click on the Publish button. To remove a page from the

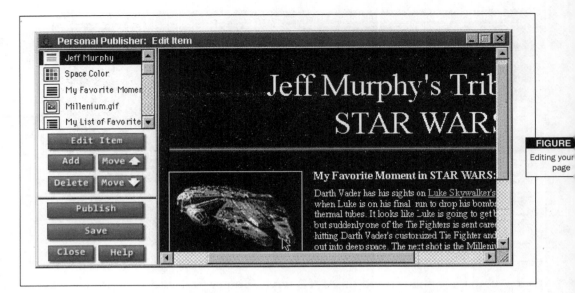

FIGURE
Editing your
page

server and place it on your "Unpublished Pages on the Your Computer"
list, select an item from the "Your Published Web Pages on AOL" list and
click on the Unpublish button.

- **Preview pages.** To preview unpublished pages, select an item from one of
  the lists and click on the Preview button.

- **Edit pages.** To edit a page, select an item from a list and click on the Edit
  button. Personal Publisher launches and displays the page for you so you
  can change, add, edit, and delete items.

- **Options/Menu.** You can link all of your pages together by creating a list of
  all links at the bottom of each Web page. To create a list of links, click on
  the Options button, then select the Menu option. This makes it easier for
  visitors to find all of your Web pages.

- **Options/Browse.** The Browse option lets you add HTML documents
  you've created with other Web page authoring tools to your directory of
  unpublished Web pages. From there you can publish them to your Web
  site. To add your Web pages, click on the Options button, select Browse,
  then select the ones you want to add to your site. Make sure these files are

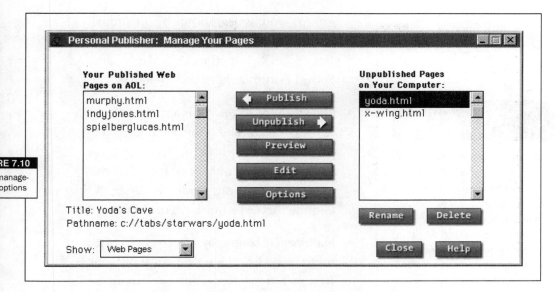

RE 7.10
manage-
options

stored in the same Web directory as your Personal Publisher pages. Otherwise, the internal links might not work.

- **Options/FTP.** The FTP option lets you upload files from any directory on your computer to your Web site space at My Place (keyword: **My Place**). To enable your FTP option, click on the Options button, then select FTP. You need to go online before you can upload FTP files.

Adding Multimedia

You don't need a lot of technical knowledge or expensive equipment to spice up your Web pages with a little multimedia. Animation, video, and sound make your Web site great entertainment for your visitors. Create your own multimedia files or use existing files from the AOL service. Note: New features are added periodically, so be sure to check the help areas within Personal Publisher for the latest information.

Here are just a few ideas for how you can add multimedia elements to your Web site:

- **Interactive movie reviews.** If you love movies and want to review them on your Web page, you can become an online Siskel and Ebert.

- **Start an online music 'zine.** AOL abounds with music clips for just about every musical taste. Give your readers an earful of the bands or musical

94

groups you write about by including sound clips with your reviews and articles. Check out the PC Music and Sound Forum at keyword **PC Music**.

- **Animate your pages.** GIF animations are easy to create and they liven up your pages. You can build a mini-cartoon with an action sequence or flash favorite pictures. Find out more at the PC Graphic Arts Forum (keyword: **PGR**).

- **Multimedia biography.** Record favorite moments—like Jenny's first words or Johnny's first steps—and add them to your Web page for less money and effort than you might think.

If you use other people's files on your pages, give the author credit on your page and a link to their Web page or e-mail address. In addition, *unless the Web page or area where you got the file explicitly gives visitors permission to use files, e-mail the author for permission.*

For more information and ideas about working with multimedia, see chapter 6.

Animated GIFs

You've probably seen Web pages featuring playful kittens scampering across the screen, e-mail links with mailboxes that open and close, and digital pictures that change every few seconds. But did you know that these are GIF animations, and you can easily create and add your own to your Web pages? GIF animations are like traditional cell animations or cartoons. First, you create or gather the digital pictures you want to use and convert them to GIF files with a program like PaintShop Pro or NeoPaint. Then you assemble your animation in a program like GIF Construction Set. GIF Construction Set's user-friendly Animation Wizard guides you through the steps. You can then use the program's preview feature to view your animation and make sure it looks right.

When you finish creating an animation file, save it to your Web folder with the GIF filename extension and insert it into your Web page the same way you would insert an ordinary GIF or JPEG image. To download the software you need, visit the Download Software area (keyword: **Software**). You can also visit the PC Graphic Arts Forum (keyword: **PGR**) for samples, help, and animated GIF-related information.

Adding Sound and Video

Adding sound and video to your Web pages is easy and fun. You can download audio and video files or create them yourself. Chapter 6 suggests inexpensive hardware and software to purchase. There are also software programs you can use to transform digital pictures into video presentations. Once you have your multimedia files, you can add them to your page by making a link to them. When a visitor clicks on your link, the appropriate application launches and plays back the file. To link to a multimedia file, place the file in your Web site folder, then create the link in Personal Publisher as you normally would. Make sure to select the Type a URL linking option. When the dialogue box appears, you can enter the filename of your multimedia file.

If you're willing to learn a little more about Web page authoring, you can also easily add a background sound to your page, or embed an AVI movie in your page that automatically plays when the page loads. To add these features, you'll need to open your HTML file in NotePad (the text editor that comes with Windows 95) and enter a line or two of HTML source code yourself. Fortunately, HTML is easy to learn and you can find plenty of online resources to help you get the hang of it. The AOL Store also offers books on the subject.

- **Adding a background sound.** You can add a sound track that will automatically play when people visit your page. To add a background sound to your Web page, open your HTML document and enter the following source code: `<BGSOUND SRC = "sound.wav" LOOP = 5>`. This tells the browser to play a background sound, and specifies the name of the sound file and how many times the sound file should play before it stops. Place the sound file in the same folder as your HTML document.

- **Adding a background video.** A background video appears on your page like an image and begins playing. To add a background video enter the following source code in your document: **img dynsrc = "movie.avi" width = "160" height = "120" start= "fileopen" controls**. This tells the browser to play a background video, and specifies the name of the movie. In addition, it specifies the height and width of the movie in pixels (the unit of measurement on the Web), and tells the movie to launch when the Web page is opened and to display the movie player controls. Movies on the Internet always measure either 160 x 120 pixels or 320 x 240 pixels. You can place the AVI movie in the same folder as your HTML files.

Before you add multimedia to your Web site, remember that sound and video files are fairly large—they can fill up your personal Web space pretty quickly, and can also take time for visitors to download. To learn more about HTML, the Web, and how it all works, see the "Web Page Help and Resources" section later in this chapter.

Multimedia File Formats

You've probably already noticed that AOL abounds with all different kinds of multimedia files. But what are they, how do they work, and what do you need to play them? You may never have to answer these questions. Just about everything you need has been built into your browser, so you can sit back and enjoy the experience. Or, you can easily find what you need at the Multimedia showcase (keyword: **mm showcase**). However, knowing how multimedia works online can help you make better use of it. Some types of files can be handled directly by the browser. Others require plug-ins or ActiveX controls—small programs that extend your browser's capabilities and enable it to handle different kinds of files.

Listed below are the most popular types of multimedia files and the plug-ins or active controls required to play them.

- **WAV.** A basic Windows sound file format. You can play back WAV files with the Media Player application that comes with Windows 95.

- **AVI.** A basic Windows video file format. You can play back AVI movies with the Media Player application that comes with Windows 95.

- **VDOLive.** VDONet's software and video file format lets multimedia developers deliver high-quality videos and broadcasts online. You can play back VDONet videos using VDOLive.

- **RealPlayer.** This Progressive Networks technology lets multimedia developers broadcast video and audio over the Web. You can play these broadcasts with RealPlayer.

- **Shockwave Flash.** With this application you can view exciting multimedia presentations, games, demonstrations, and movies created with Macromedia's high-end multimedia applications like Director and Author Ware.

Most people have to download and install plug-ins and ActiveX controls themselves. Fortunately, AOL comes with the most popular ones already installed.

Web Page Help and Resources

Personal Publisher gives you a great way to get started with Web publishing. But where do you go when you want to add more features to your Web site? Online, of course. AOL abounds with areas that discuss sound, video, multimedia, graphics,

FIGURE 7.11

Multimedia Showcase

digital pictures, and desktop publishing. You'll find information, examples, and tutorials, along with experts ready to give you help and advice.

Here are a few places you can visit for information about Web publishing, digital pictures, and multimedia:

- **On the Net.** If you're looking for classes and tools and a good all-purpose resource, try keyword **On the Net**.

- **The Sound Room.** Enter the keyword **Sound Room** to access entire libraries full of sound files and information that you can download, listen to, and use. A built-in sound player lets you listen to files online before you download them.

- **Desktop Cinema.** Browse through the video libraries and find exciting videos for your Web site. The area also has a built-in video player so you can view the movies online. Enter the keyword **Sound Room** and click on Desktop Cinema.

- **Multimedia Showcase.** Visit this multimedia mecca for information, downloadable files, contests, creative inspiration, featured sites, and more. Enter the keyword **mm showcase**, or visit the Web page shown in figure 7.11 (http://multimedia.aol.com).

- **Web Page Clip Art Creation Center.** Learn about how to create and format artwork for your Web pages, including background textures, animated GIFs, and more. The Web Page Clip Art Creation Center (keyword: **Webart**) guides you to resources and artwork you can use.

- **Desktop and Web Publishing forum.** Aspiring Web publishers can find lots of useful resources from this forum (keyword: **MDWP**), including HTML support and downloadable fonts.

Use these resources to find just the right sound clip, video file, or clip art for your Web page, or learn about exciting new things you can do to enhance your Web pages.

8

KIDS AND DIGITAL PICTURES

Now that you're becoming a digital pictures expert, you can start encouraging your children to use them too. Kids have lots of creativity, and digital pictures can help them bring their ideas to life. They can dress up school reports with photographs, maps, and works of art; create official-looking ID cards for clubs and school activities; publish their own Web page or newsletter; create greeting cards for birthdays and holidays. They can also meet other creative kids online and learn from them, and access a multitude of online resources for their projects.

This chapter describes online places where kids can go for fun, education, ideas, and encouragement—and how you can help keep them out of trouble. Then, the chapter introduces you to some fun and educational projects that can keep your kids happily busy.

Here are a few ways that your kids can use digital pictures:

- **Researching school reports.** Digital pictures can make your children more interested in schoolwork, while making their schoolwork more interesting. Your children can find a wealth of information and pictures on the AOL service that they won't find in their textbook.

- **Entering contests.** Does Tracy get in trouble for doodling in class? Encourage her to enter an online art contest. Blackberry Creek (keyword: **Blackberry**) and other areas invite your children to submit artwork, scrapbooks, and photographs for contests on a regular basis, and show the winners' work online.

- **Making new friends.** Communicating online brings back many of the old-fashioned pleasures of letter writing. If Michael seems shy around people, encourage him to make friends online. He can correspond with kids from around the world, meet other kids who share the same interests and concerns, and exchange digital pictures with them.

- **Helping others.** Does Susie talk about the environment a lot? Does Frank constantly nag you to quit smoking? Does Jeannie ask questions about homeless people every time you take her to the city? Many of today's kids are concerned about social issues. They can go online to learn more and find out how they can help, or create a Web page with digital pictures to voice their concerns and encourage other people to think about them.

- **Creating special projects.** Creative kids sometimes have trouble finishing projects when they don't turn out the way they imagined them. With digital pictures and today's software, it's easy for kids to create slick-looking newsletters, greeting cards, Web pages, and just about anything they can think of.

Protecting Your Kids Online

Sure you want your kids to have fun on AOL and the Internet, and to use their resources for school and creative projects. But like many parents, you may be concerned about the possibility that they might be exposed to unsuitable material. Fortunately, there are plenty of places online that are geared especially to children's interests and needs. For example, the Kids Only channel (keyword: **Kids Only**), shown in figure 8.1, offers a variety of activities and material especially for kids.

In addition, you can use AOL's built-in Parental Controls to limit your children's online access to areas appropriate for their age group and your family's values. The Parental Controls features let you select options for what types of sites your kids can access, and who they can communicate with. Depending on your children's age and maturity, you can customize your Parental Controls settings so that you can, for example, allow your teenager more freedom than you allow your first-grader. If you'd like to see exactly what your children will experience while they're online, log on as one of your children, then try to access sites and surf the Web.

FIGURE 8.1
Kids Only

To set Parental Controls:

1. Click on the My AOL toolbar button and select Parental Controls from the list.

2. When the Parental Controls dialogue box appears, as shown in figure 8.2, click on Create a Screen Name to display options for setting up screen names for each member of your family.

3. When you finish creating screen names, return to the Parental Controls dialogue box. A list of screen names appears on the Secondary accounts list.

4. Select a screen name and click on the Custom Controls button.

5. When the Custom Controls dialogue box appears, as shown in figure 8.3, specify Web controls by selecting an item from the list, reading the explanation and instructions in the scrolling text area, and clicking on the Web Controls button.

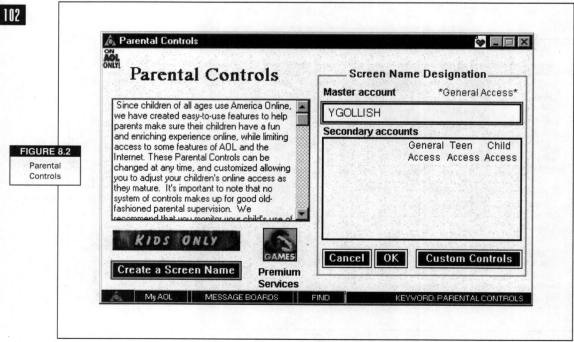

FIGURE 8.2

Parental
Controls

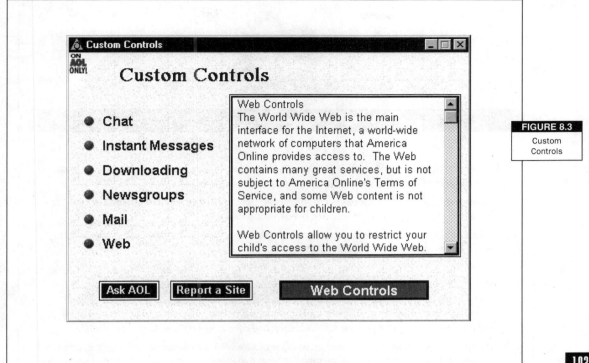

FIGURE 8.3

Custom
Controls

103

(Note: Although the 4.0 software was being finalized as we wrote this, AOL had planned to include a Parental Controls button right on the Welcome screen.)

Once you've set your Parental Controls, you can feel reasonably secure about your children's online journeys. However, it is also important for you to talk with your children about online safety—just as you tell them to look both ways when crossing the street on the way to school. Talking to them about their online safety is as important as talking to them about their safety in the real world. Encourage them to ask questions and to talk to you if they encounter anything that makes them feel funny or uncomfortable. If you're not sure where to begin, take a look at the safety tips in the Kids Only area. Be sure to warn them *never* to give out personal information, like your address, to people they meet online.

With all that said, most kids have positive online experiences, and get a lot out of using the AOL service and participating in its communities.

There are many wolves and traps lurking online for children. Following are some safety tips you can discuss with your children and post for them to see when they are online.

1. Never give your AOL or other password to anyone. Don't even give your password to a friend or someone who says he is from AOL and needs your password.

2. Do not tell anyone your home address or phone number. If you want to give your address to a friend online, ask a parent's permission first.

3. Never agree to meet with anyone in person. If someone asks to meet you, tell a parent and ask permission.

4. Anytime you feel threatened, funny, or uncomfortable about anything someone does or says online, tell your parents. If someone uses threatening or bad language with you, tell your parents. Remember, you have the option of turning the computer *off* if you feel uncomfortable.

5. If anyone uses bad language or makes you feel unsafe while you're online, call a guide. Use the keyword **KO Help** to notify a guide and tell her what happened. You can also leave the chat room where the offending person is or sign off the AOL service altogether.

6. Never accept anything from a stranger. This includes files, Web page addresses or URLs, or e-mail.

Activities and Projects for Kids

Before you begin trying to teach your children how to use a computer, watch out! They might already know more than you. Today's kids often learn how to use computers at school at an early age. Whether Johnny's a junior computer whiz or doesn't know a keyboard from a key ring, you can still encourage him to use digital pictures and online resources productively. The following sections suggest a few projects and offer tips and suggestions for keeping your children challenged and busy.

Some children may seem overwhelmed or reluctant at first. You can get them excited by going online and showing them projects that other kids have created. Or try brainstorming with them to come up with a few ideas, and then narrow the list. You can start off with something small, like a Mother's Day card for Grandma.

A final word of advice: don't let your expectations ruin the fun. Sure, you'd like Alex to get cracking on that school report. But if he would rather design a Michael Jordan Web page, let him. As he gets used to working with digital pictures and sees all the neat things he can do with them, he'll start using them for homework too.

Creating Web Pages

Your children may look over your shoulder while you create your Web page—or even help you and make suggestions. They probably want to create a home page of their own. After all, many of their friends have Web pages. With AOL, each member of your family, including the dog, can have his own Web site. Your account gives you 10 MB of personal Web page space that can be distributed into individual 2 MB areas for each screen name in your family.

Your children are probably bursting with ideas about what they want to include on their Web page and how they want their page to look. Sit down with them, help them plan out their page, and show them other kids' Web sites to give them more ideas. You can also help them gather digital pictures and explain how to use the Picture Gallery. If Lisa likes horses, encourage her to do a little research and create an interesting and visually appealing page about horses. If Jimmy likes to go fishing with Dad, help him pick out pictures and write up some fun fishing stories and add fish-related trivia.

Posting Artwork Online

Kids always seem to be drawing, writing stories, building models, or working on crafts. Sometimes they start these projects in school, sometimes they dream things up on their own. No matter where the ideas come from, kids enjoy showing people their creations. Kids Only has several places where kids can display their masterpieces for other kids to see. Blackberry Creek also frequently requests projects from children, and sponsors contests with prizes.

Help your children come up with ideas for things they can create and display as artwork in one of these Kids Only areas. Kids can use the image programs discussed in chapter 11 to create a montage of digital pictures of their pets, their favorite artwork, or a self-portrait. Or, you can show them how to scan their drawings or take pictures of their crafts. If Claire and her friends love dressing up and playacting, encourage them to write a screenplay, take a picture of each part of the story, then assemble the pictures and add a narration.

Spiffing Up Homework

Every kid has homework, but not all of them want to do it. Help them use digital pictures to make their homework more interesting. Most word processing programs let you insert digital pictures in the text and create tables and charts. If Diane has to write a report on Bulgaria or South Dakota, she can find informative pictures—like the state flag and local scenes and activities—to add to her report. Have Kevin use photographs and clip art to create more interesting diagrams and charts for science and math classes—the pictures may also help him understand the material better.

Your kids can also visit the Ask-A-Teacher area (keyword: **Homework Help**) to find teachers, tutors, and other kids to help them with their homework. Or they can get together with other kids who study the same subject and start a Homework Help club. They can make up rules for the club and display their spiffed-up homework on the club message board.

Newsletters

If Cory loves to write, suggest he get together with online and offline pals and start a newsletter. Digital pictures, word processing software, and today's inexpensive printers make it easy for kids to create good-looking publications of their own, like the one shown in figure 8.4. A newsletter can focus on anything under the sun, from what's happening in the neighborhood to information related to a club, hobby, or area of interest. Or he can publish a poetry or art journal showcasing his own or his friends' work.

Your child can print her publication on paper and pass it around, send it to people via e-mail, publish it as a Web page, or all of the above. E-mail, Instant Messages, and forum message boards also give kids a great way to plan the next issue and brainstorm on articles. But remember that publishing a newsletter is a big undertaking. Help Shelby plan and organize it so she can manage and learn from the experience.

Club Materials

Most children love to join clubs. Whether they participate in organized activities or create a club with a group of friends, they enjoy the activities, the sense of belong-

FIGURE 8.4

A newsletter created in Microsoft Word

ing, and the chance to take initiative and use their unique talents. With digital pictures and your computer, your children can create all kinds of materials their clubs can use, including personalized ID cards, secret rule books, and newsletters. Many of the techniques needed for creating these materials have been covered in previous chapters. You can use what you've learned to help your children learn too.

Here are some ideas for club materials:

- **Personalized ID cards.** Your child can instruct the other members to provide small pictures of themselves (school pictures work just fine) on disk. He can use a word processor to create a table. Each table cell can include a picture of a member, along with her name and other information. He can also experiment with special fonts and colors (if you have a color printer). He can print the finished document on cardstock, then use a paper cutter to separate the ID cards.

- **Rule books.** No club is worth joining if it doesn't have a secret rule book. First, have your children confer with other club members about what secret rules they want. Then they can use the AOL text editor to type rules, adding clip art and photographs from the Picture Gallery. If all of the club members are online, your child can also set up the rule book in an e-mail message and send it to everyone.

- **Club newsletters.** Your child can volunteer to be the editor of the club's newsletter. She can feature a club member of the month or week with a digital picture of the member and his profile. She can write up club news and include digital pictures of events. She can also use clip art to break up the text and make a more entertaining and visually pleasing layout.

- **Personalized yearbooks.** Like you, your children have their favorite chat rooms. They form bonds in those rooms and make lasting friendships. In school, your older children can buy a yearbook as a remembrance of the good times they had. They can create something similar for their clubs, or for their chat room friends. Through the year, your children can collect digital pictures, stories, and information about the other kids in the club or chat room. The yearbook can also include standard yearbook fare, such as Most Likely to Succeed and Featured Moments.

The ideas and suggestions in this chapter will help your children keep busy and stimulate their minds. These projects are also a great way for you and your children to spend quality time together.

9

USING DIGITAL PICTURES AT WORK

We associate pictures with fun or special occasions. But digital pictures can also help you be more productive and promote your business. You already use pictures at work every day without even thinking about it. Take a look at the stationery you print your correspondence on and the business cards you hand out. They probably have a logo or other graphic element. Your sales brochures and company literature may include photographs or clip art.

Perhaps you would like to use more images in your materials, but haven't yet because you think doing so is too costly, or requires too much time or technical skill. Fortunately, today's technology makes it easy and inexpensive to create and distribute attractive materials including digital pictures. You have America Online, inexpensive hardware and software, and your newly acquired digital pictures expertise at your disposal. Whether your business earns you six figures or you run a shoestring startup out of your house, digital pictures can help you get the word out, impress clients and customers, get things done faster, and improve your existing materials.

This chapter introduces you to a variety of ways to use digital pictures—online and off—to benefit your business:

- **Be your own designer and printer.** An inexpensive color printer and a good word processing or desktop publishing program can help you quickly design your own materials and print them out when you need them. Even if you already work with a graphic designer, good software and a color printer give you the flexibility to customize and update files at a moment's notice. You can find them in the Digital Imaging Shop of the AOL Store (keyword: **Digital Shop**).

- **Track clients, inventory, and business records.** Digital pictures provide memory cues that can help you stay organized and remember all those details. Many commonly used database, personal management, and other office productivity software programs let you import digital pictures.

This chapter will clue you in on all the ways you can use digital pictures at work. Use them on business cards, stationery, sales brochures, catalogs, and other materials. Use them to impress clients and maintain contact with them online. Use them to track your customers, inventory, and business records.

Create Your Own Business Materials

Printing takes up a sizable chunk of everyone's business budget. Wouldn't it be great to find a way to reduce costs? With digital pictures, clip art, and a color printer, you can save money, gain flexibility, and have a little fun creating your own business materials. This is much easier than you may think.

Judith and Bob run a small, specialty gift shop. For years they made a comfortable living from business generated by their Yellow Pages and local newspaper ads. Then they started visiting the AOL WorkPlace channel (keyword: **Workplace**), as shown in figure 9.1.

They found forums, e-mail lists, and other resources for information and support in running their small business. In addition to making some wonderful friends and contacts on these forums and lists, they learned about scanners and color printers, and how other entrepreneurs use them. Now Judith and Bob design and print invitations to the store's holiday party, flyers for upcoming sales, greeting cards for special customers, and other special pieces. Sure, they still send big jobs to the printer. But before the advent of inexpensive color printers, Judith and Bob never could have afforded to print the kind of gorgeous, full-color brochures that bring in slews of new customers.

FIGURE 9.1

WorkPlace Main Screen

No matter what kind of business you run, there are times when tailoring a proposal or brochure for a particular client is very useful. Or what about the time you moved to a new location and had to change all your business cards and letterhead, though you still had hundreds left from the last print run? With digital pictures and the equipment discussed in chapter 10, you can design attractive pieces on the fly. If you're just starting out and aren't yet ready to spend money having a printer make up 1,000 business cards, you can also print out professional-looking cards as you need them.

Business Cards

A business card may be small, yet this simple piece of paper says more about your company and goes farther in promoting your business than almost any other tool you use. When you send a letter to a client, you sometimes slip one of your business cards inside. Every meeting you attend seems to begin or end with participants passing out business cards. Business cards with color and graphics get the most attention. But until now most of us could afford only the plain old black-and-white ones. Now you can hand out exciting-looking, colorful business cards with digital pictures—even if you don't have a color printer.

First, visit an office supply store and purchase pre-made packages of business cards. Pre-made business cards come in sheets of thick paper stock still thin enough to run through your printer. The paper is perforated so you can separate the cards from one another after you finish printing them. Each sheet of paper yields ten business cards. They come in all different colors. Some even come with colorful designs already printed on them.

After purchasing your business cards, you can create a set of cards with your word processor or desktop publishing program. Digital pictures can go a long way when personalizing your card. You can use either clip art or a simple photograph. If you use a photograph, use an image that looks good even when reduced in size.

Many programs come with templates for generating business cards. Or you can create your own template using the following specifications:

- **Margins.** Set the top, bottom, right, and left margins to .5 inches.

- **Columns.** Create two columns with a column width of .25 inches each.

- **Height and width.** Each card on the sheet of paper is 2 inches high and 3.5 inches wide. Leave a little space between each card.

Experiment with fonts and pictures until you design a business card you like. Then copy and paste it to create your sheet of business cards. Each column should have five cards for a total of ten. Some word processing programs make it easy for you to set up business cards. They let you create, size, and position frames that enclose text and images. You can then copy, paste, and position each frame. With other programs, you may have to experiment until your cards are positioned correctly for printing.

Letterhead

John is an accountant working from his home office. Although he considers himself more of a number cruncher than an artistic type, he still likes his stationery, business cards, and other materials to stand out from the crowd. With some clip art and a

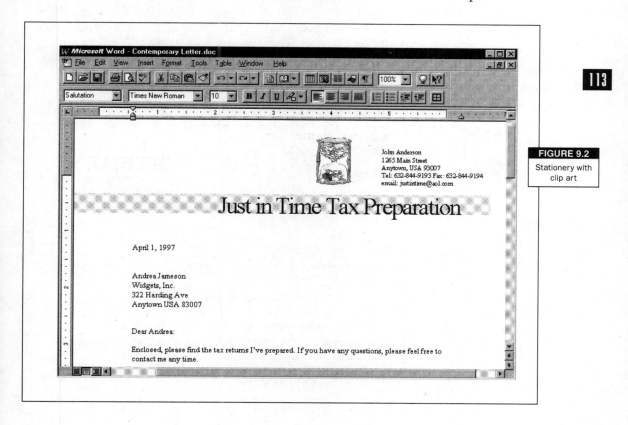

FIGURE 9.2
Stationery with clip art

template, John created his own stationery, as shown in figure 9.2. He then bought some good paper stock and matching envelopes for his correspondence, and gets lots of comments on how nice his stationery looks. When his wife gave him a digital camera for his birthday, John was surprised by how much he enjoyed working with digital pictures. Now he designs his own holiday cards, tax-time reminder notices, and other mailings.

Making your own stationery is even easier than making your own business cards. Buy paper you like in a variety of colors and stocks. Many stores even sell sets of pre-made business cards, stationery, and envelopes so all your materials will match. Then use a template in your desktop publishing or word processing program and insert your images and information (see figure 9.3). Or you can create the letterhead from scratch.

Brochures, Reports, and Proposals

Once you get the hang of working with text and images, you can start using digital pictures in other areas of your business. Mark, a sales manager, often brings work home with him. One night, after tucking his kids into bed, he had only a couple of hours in which to crank out a sales report for the next day's meeting and still have time for a decent night's sleep. Mark's department had done particularly well over

114

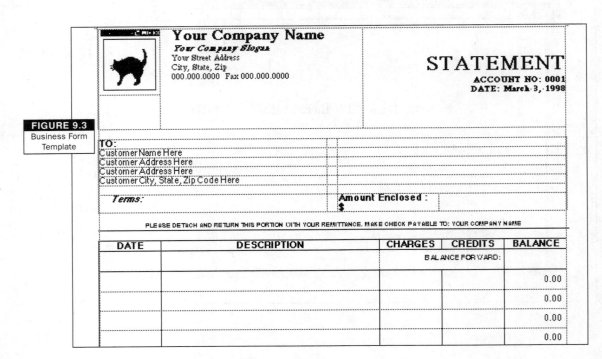

FIGURE 9.3
Business Form
Template

the past fiscal quarter and he wanted upper-level managers to notice.

First, he wrote the report. Then he scanned in photographs of the booth he and his department set up at a recent trade show, the sales person of the month, and other recent events. He also used clip art to jazz up the graphs and charts. By the end of the evening, Mark had a stack of impressive-looking color printouts in time to get plenty of sleep for the next day's meeting.

Presentation Transparencies

Karen was making a Tuesday presentation to one of the biggest manufacturers in her territory. She knew pictures would convince their board of directors that her company's products are the best for their business. She scanned pictures of other companies using her products, illustrating the different ways they can be used. Then she used the digital pictures and her computer to put together a dynamite presentation. Once each page of her presentation was perfect, she printed copies on her company's color printer. Then she used those copies and her company's color copier to make transparencies.

All weekend Karen practiced her presentation until she had it down perfectly for the Tuesday meeting. Her confidence came through in her presentation. She impressed the board and got their business.

Jim is a contract speaker. He works for a national company that books him for conferences and seminars all over the country. He is considered an expert in his field and his seminars are always booked to capacity. Jim knows if he spent the whole eight hours of each presentation just speaking, he would

COMPRESSING FILES FOR QUICK AND EASY TRANSFER AND STORAGE

Certain digital formats compress photo images well. However, no matter what digital format you use, digital picture files are larger than other types of files because of the amount of information they contain.

When you try to send these files via e-mail or Instant Messages, the transfer can take several minutes. Compressing your digital picture files before you send them will save you and the recipient time. That's why AOL 4.0 has been designed to compress multiple file attachments automatically.

If you want to transfer or store digital pictures online, you need to compress them into smaller files. Several programs compress, or zip, files for you. One such program, mentioned in an earlier chapter, is called WinZip. It is a shareware program; that means you pay a small fee to obtain a registered copy of the program. You can find it at the Software Center (keyword: **Software**).

115

lose his audience. So he scans relevant photographs into his computer, prints them on his color printer, and converts them into transparencies at a print shop for less than $5 each. He uses the slide show to boost his presentation.

With the proper equipment and tools, a little imagination, and initiative, you can create killer transparencies using digital pictures. Look for tools like a color printer, a color copier, a scanner, and a digital camera at the AOL Store (keyword: **AOL Store**).

Promoting Your Business Online

Insiders know AOL and the Web offer a wealth of business opportunities. Beverly runs a business developing custom applications and help systems for small businesses. Five years ago she signed up with AOL, and since then her business has doubled. Although some chat groups and forums discourage advertising, on others it is perfectly acceptable. Beverly finds that when she mentions what she does, people sometimes send e-mail messages asking about her services and rates. When she writes back, she includes an electronic business card so people will remember her. And of course, her Web page, with links to clients she has worked for, helps generate business for her too.

You too can use AOL as an easy way to distribute digital pictures and other types of files. If you run a restaurant and people you meet online ask about it, you can e-mail them pictures of your location and cuisine. Who knows? They may actually travel to your area sometime. Or, if you're a professional photographer, you can upload pictures of your work to designated forums or display them on your Web page.

E-mail

We take e-mail so much for granted, many of us don't even think of it as a business tool. E-mail gives you an easy way to send digital pictures and other types of files back and forth. Suppose you are a freelance writer who has discovered a wonderful, sleepy beach town on the California coast. If you are inspired, you could go online to find the Web sites of a few magazines likely to print an article about it. Look for the editors' e-mail addresses and send query letters. Later, you can send the article and a couple of pictures as e-mail attachments.

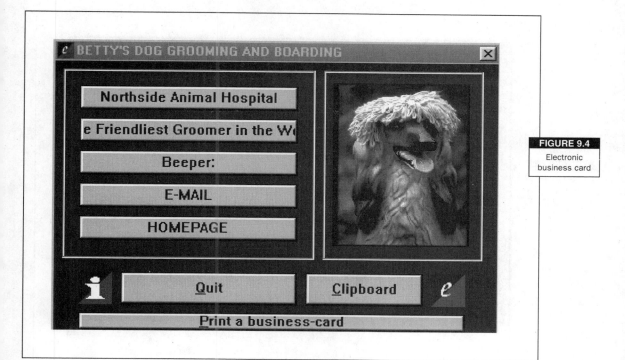

FIGURE 9.4

Electronic
business card

Inside the figure:

BETTY'S DOG GROOMING AND BOARDING ✕

Northside Animal Hospital

e Friendliest Groomer in the Wo

Beeper:

E-MAIL

HOMEPAGE

Quit   Clipboard

Print a business-card

Electronic Business Cards

Sam runs a small mail order catalog business. He learned how to create an electronic business card and attaches it to his e-mail correspondence and forum postings. Betty is a dog groomer who also arranges for care and boarding of people's pets. She loves giving fellow members of the AOL community tips on grooming and caring for pets and regularly exchanges electronic business cards with the people she meets online (see figure 9.4). Electronic business cards make it easy to provide people with contact information and make an impression in your online communications.

Electronic business card programs like Visual Business Cards and Electronic Card Maker let other people view your business card—even if they don't have the program you used to create it. Some of these applications are shareware, so you can try them before you buy them.

FIGURE 9.5

A small business
Web page

118

Electronic business card applications generally display a form where you enter your name, company name, contact information, and a picture. Sometimes you can even include a sound file. Once you finish creating the business card, save it as a file or copy it to your computer's clipboard so you can paste it into other files. When you attach it to messages, your recipients can open the file and view it. Some programs display all the information, while others require the user to click on buttons to display the information associated with the button. Electronic business cards only work online. They do not print correctly as typical business cards.

Web Pages

Let's say you're the brand-new proprietor of a quaint bed-and-breakfast. How can you attract more guests? Try creating a Web page like the one shown in figure 9.5. Each lovely, cozy room is displayed to entice customers to book reservations. You can use banner ads to advertise your inn and Web site on other sites. Or contact people in related businesses—such as vacation and travel—to list links on each other's pages. Naturally, you can register your Web site with all of the search engines, starting with AOL NetFind, which you can select from the menu that appears when you click on the Internet button on the AOL toolbar. Each search engine has an area where you can register your Web site, and provides detailed instructions to make the process easy.

Tracking Clients and Inventory

You can also use digital pictures to help track clients and inventory. For example, Terry and Jeanne own a small but successful nursery and landscaping business. Like most of us, they need to stay competitive, but they don't have a large operating or advertising budget. Digital pictures help them make the most of their limited resources. Terry is a photography buff and he takes digital pictures the minute flowers bloom or new plants arrive. Like him, you can take digital pictures of your inventory and upload them for your customers to see.

Microsoft Access and several other popular database programs let you import pictures into your files, where you can use them to locate products for particular customers.

Once you've imported the pictures into your database, you can easily find the pictures and related information for your company's online catalog. Terry and Jeanne's Web site has become so popular among gardening enthusiasts that they can barely keep up with their online orders.

Keeping track of everything happening in your business is essential for success. Besides, the IRS requires that you keep accurate records of all financial transactions. To file an accurate tax return, you must know your inventory, your sales, and your receipts.

Or let's say you need to keep track of a *lot* of inventory and plan to publish a catalog. Kathy and Steve run a mail-order catalog for specialty pet products. They publish their catalog four times a year. Finding the right pictures for the listings was a hassle until Kathy began using a scanner and digital camera. By adding her own pictures to the company's inventory database, she made gathering and organizing material for the catalog a whole lot easier.

Digital pictures can even help you keep on top of smaller operations. For example, when Mary Ann signs on a new client for her personal shopping business, the client gives her pictures of everyone on his gift list. Mary Ann then converts the pictures to digital format, if needed, and adds them to a customer tracking program. Her personal scheduling program reminds her to shop for a client. Then she finds the client in her database, where she reviews the client's needs, past gifts given (also shown as digital pictures), and the date the gift must be delivered. With all the information Mary Ann has in her client database, she is an informed shopper who can purchase the perfect gift for her client. She looks good and the client looks even better to his special someone. Birthdays and anniversaries are never forgotten and Mary Ann never makes the mistake of buying the wrong present for the wrong person or sending a duplicate present.

Is your head starting to be filled with creative ideas for digital pictures? If so, you will probably want to consider setting up a digital lab. We'll show you how in the next chapter.

10
HOW TO SET UP A HOME DIGITAL LAB

Now that you know how digital imaging makes it easy for you to create, edit, and share pictures through your computer, you might want to set up a home digital imaging lab. It's easier and cheaper than ever before. Digital pictures are cheaper because of newly affordable, high-quality color ink-jet printers, scanners, and the lower-cost digital cameras. Other imaging tools like digital video cameras, handheld image capturing devices, and desktop scanners are also cheaper and readily available. You can combine any or all of these to create your own digital imaging lab.

This chapter tells you how to set up a digital lab. But if you prefer to experiment with the technology first, you still have another option. You can take a roll of film to a film lab and have your pictures developed and the images transferred to a floppy disk or a photo CD. This only costs a couple of dollars more than developing a roll the normal way. You can then insert the CD or disk in your CD-ROM drive, view your pictures in the Picture Gallery or another image editing program, select the ones you want, save them to your computer, and work with them. Sending your film to a lab involves a two-week turnaround, or longer. So you won't have the flexibility and convenience of a home digital lab. It does allow you to get a feel for the technology and its potential.

If you don't know which lab to send your film to, visit Mystic Color Labs by entering the keyword **MCL**. They have an online form you can fill out for more information. In less than a week, you'll receive a starter kit with instructions, prices, a photo mailer, and a special discount for new customers. Mystic Color Labs also offers a service called PC Photos. They can send your pictures on disk or you can cut down on mailing time by arranging to download your pictures from Mystic's Internet site.

Whether you have a home office or simply wish to work on projects with the kids, the great projects in this book are all easier to execute with a digital lab. Your documents can be ready the same day you think them up by using the tools described in this chapter.

Digital imaging lets you be spontaneous. If you're walking around town with a digital camera and capture an image you really like, print it out using a new, photo-quality ink-jet printer and share the image with your friends and family within minutes. No more waiting for the film to be developed.

Some of the devices you'll get acquainted with in this chapter are:

- Desktop or flatbed scanners

- Digital cameras

- Low-cost digital video cameras

- Photo-quality ink-jet printers

- Writable CD-ROMs, removable drives, and large hard drives

- Backup devices

- High-speed video cards

You can learn more about them at the Hardware Shop in the AOL Store (keyword: **Hardware Center**).

Understanding Personal Image Capturing

"Personal image capturing" is a fancy term for "taking your own digital pictures." It's also a booming area in computer graphics. The sheer variety of devices you can use for capturing and processing images is bewildering. To have a reasonably versatile personal imaging system, you'll need two key devices: a color ink-jet printer and a digital camera. These items are two of the best-selling computer graphics products, and the cheapest way to get started. Anything else you want, like perhaps a scanner, will just extend your capabilities in new directions. Fortunately, image devices are easy to connect to your system. Most of them come with special cables and detailed instructions on how to hook them up to your computer.

123

Where Do I Start?

Start thinking of your computer as your new digital lab. It "develops" and displays your images, and also helps you edit, lay out, and output them. If you're running a fairly new system with Windows 95, you should already have many of the tools you need. Most of the newer machines come with sound and video cards that can handle digital sounds and images. Every new system made within the last two or three years also comes with a CD-ROM drive. As we show later, you'll still need some additional hardware and software to set up your digital lab. You can find them at the Digital Imaging and Software Shops in the AOL Store.

Imaging does require space on your computer. Image files take up a lot of room on your system, so you may need a large hard drive and a way to back up your files. If your system has only 200 to 500 MB of disk space, that's not going to be enough and it may be time to upgrade. Fortunately, hard disk space is cheap, especially compared to what it was a few years ago.

How Does All This Stuff Work?

Digital image devices capture images—either by scanning a photograph, taking a picture, or grabbing a video frame—and convert them to a format your computer can understand. The digital image device is the translator between the computer (digital) and "real" (analog) world. However, the digital quality of your pictures means they may not always look quite the way you expect. *Resolution* is the key term you'll need to remember from this chapter, and it applies to just about everything concerning digital pictures.

Many personal imaging applications define resolution using pixels. What is a pixel? The word stands for picture element. They're the tiny dots that everything displayed on your computer screen is composed of. Printers, on the other hand, define resolution in dots per inch (dpi). The higher the resolution, the higher the image quality you get.

Scanners

If you need to print lots of flyers, or other materials, a scanner can prove invaluable. Take Kay, for example. She's a real-estate agent at a firm in a small country town popular with tourists. Her town has a steady turnover in house sales. Until now, she's had to take photographs of homes going onto the market, get the film developed, and take the photos to a graphic designer who scans the photos and produces simple flyers for showing the properties to prospective buyers. (When she's feeling ambitious, she might have her photos placed on a photo CD, but that drives up the cost and the time factor.) She has to do this several times a week. She's also bitten the bullet and purchased a fairly expensive Pentium MMX PC to organize her work, and runs Microsoft Office as her main software for word processing and other tasks.

Kay is tired of running around every day. She works in a busy office, and the constant errand running takes its toll. What can she do to reduce her errands so she has more time to spend with her clients? And what can she do to get the most out of her computer investment? Kay needs two key tools: a decent digital camera, and a high-quality ink-jet printer. With these two simple devices, her efficiency can take a big jump.

So now Kay has purchased a good-quality digital camera and a $250 Epson color ink-jet printer. The printer hooks up easily to the computer and she's immediately printing out documents. As a test run, she takes the camera to a couple of new client homes and takes several shots of each. Instead of running to a film lab, Kay takes her camera back to the office, downloads the new images to her computer, spends five minutes touching them up with the provided software, and imports the pictures into her word processor.

After typing in information on each house, Kay sets her printer output to Best Quality and lets 'er rip. Within a few more minutes she has a new set of real estate brochures she can post in her front window and hand out to clients. The local graphics house will lose her as a client, but Kay saves the money she would have spent on them and makes more money by being available to her clients.

Scanners are an increasingly common imaging tool. Popular for years with computerized desktop publishing and graphics businesses, desktop scanners have suddenly become drastically more affordable. In fact, desktop scanners have become so cheap that they've driven other types of scanners out of the market. The biggest advantage for desktop scanners is that you can copy literally any image (a photograph, a hand-drawn picture, a page from a magazine) into your system with the touch of a button.

For the last several years, handheld scanning devices such as the Logitech ScanMan were a low-cost alternative to the more expensive desktop variety. Handheld scanners are useful primarily for scanning columns of text or small photographs. If you use an older handheld scanner to digitize graphics, you'll have to scan parts of larger images and "stitch" them together, which is difficult at best and pointless most of the time. It's also very difficult to physically hold a scanner and smoothly capture an image. Devices of this type usually lack flexibility and are essentially obsolete.

Desktop scanners, which can be purchased at prices starting under $100, are also often called *flatbed* scanners because you lay an entire page facedown on the glass scanning surface.

One disadvantage of desktop scanners is they take up more space than the old handheld type. Since they scan an entire sheet of paper (often, even a legal-size sheet) at once, they can crowd your desk. Consider getting a separate table for your scanner.

Scanner resolution is measured in dots per inch (dpi). That's because scanners have much more in common with printers than they do with digital cameras or computer screens, with resolution measured in pixels. For basic imaging purposes, you need a scanner with a minimum resolution of 300 dpi.

You'll find all low-cost scanners offer this resolution. If cost is less important than quality, consider buying a 600 dpi scanner. You'll spend about twice as much (starting under $200 and going to about $500), but image quality is better. For personal and small-business imaging, it's not usually necessary to spend that kind of money. Also bear in mind that the higher the dpi setting, the larger your scanned file will be. Scanned graphics files can be huge, especially with photographs. (For more information on what you can do about the size of your growing collection of graphics files, see the section "Understanding Storage Options" later in this chapter.)

Of course, it's not enough to just buy a scanner. You also need a way to get the image into your computer. Even the cheapest scanners provide basic software for operating them from your computer. Many of the better scanners even provide a version of Adobe Photoshop with their product, but all of them provide some way to create, edit, and manage images. Consider this feature when purchasing your scanner. The AOL Store's Digital Shop (keyword: **Digital Shop**) offers a full line of scanners from leading vendors such as Storm, Visioneer, and Umax.

Understanding Digital Cameras

Handheld digital cameras are a key reason why personal digital imaging is becoming such a popular application. A digital camera (figure 10.1) functions very like a normal camera. You carry it around just as you would a normal camera, and point-and-shoot as you normally would.

The images a digital camera captures are stored very differently, however. Those images never see film or negatives. They're stored in a special type of memory inside the camera, and downloaded to your computer when you're ready to print them out or work with them in other ways. Because no film processing is involved, you get instant gratification with a digital camera. Popular, entry-level digital cameras are made by a wide variety of manufacturers, including Kodak, Minolta, and Casio. Not surprisingly, many conventional camera manufacturers are jumping into this market with both feet.

Entry-level digital cameras cost anywhere from $150 to $500, depending on their features. The AOL Store's Digital Shop (keyword: **Digital Shop**) offers several different digital cameras in that price range. Ideally, digital cameras will have a resolution of around 640 x 480 pixels and a small LCD view screen on the back for previewing your shots before taking them.

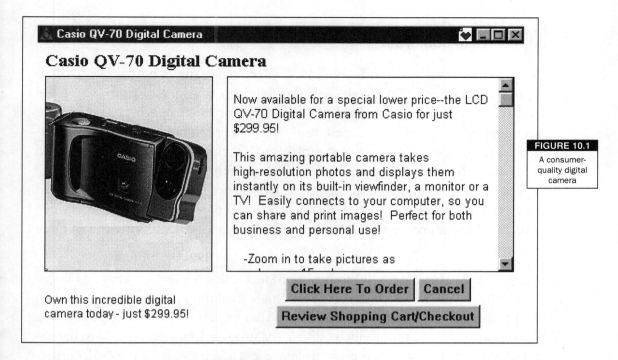

Some other tips: You should never buy a digital camera with a plastic lens. Glass lenses may drive up the cost a bit, but the camera will last a lot longer and provide much better image quality. More and more digital cameras now include zoom and flash capabilities. The flash feature is almost mandatory, with zoom being a much more costly (but desirable) option.

At the higher end of the price scale are devices known as megapixel cameras. They're so-called because they can capture digital images at higher resolutions (1024 x 768 and 1280 x 1024 pixels). Olympus, Kodak, and other manufacturers make digital cameras with higher image quality than more inexpensive brands.

You pay for this quality, both in terms of money and in the size of the graphics files those cameras generate. A very good quality megapixel digital camera will cost a bare minimum of $799 and go up substantially from there. In fact, you can spend up to $25,000 for the very best digital cameras on the market.

To get the most out of a digital camera, you're going to need a high-quality color printer. For digital camera output, a good ink-jet printer is more than adequate. Fortunately, these are cheap, common, and easy to hook up to a PC or Macintosh system. We'll talk more about ink-jet printers, in the "Producing Output" section later.

Digital Video Cameras

Billy is an insurance agent in Escondido, California. He runs a busy office. Dozens of clients sit in front of his desk every day, buying car insurance from him. Until now, Billy has had to take photographs of each car for which he writes a policy, wait three days to get the film developed, run out to the photo house to pick up the pictures, then open the files again and sort through them to add the correct photo to each policy. He's tried Polaroid pictures, but found those photos fade rapidly and are of poor quality, not to mention expensive. He wants to find a way to cut costs and ease the record-keeping process. He has a decent computer and already owns a video camera and a laser printer. Can Billy tie all these things together to solve this nagging problem?

Yes, he can. By spending $200 to buy a product called Snappy (at keyword **Digital Shop**) Billy can use his video camera to take high-resolution pictures of any car in his lot and immediately print the picture on his laser printer. Because Snappy connects the computer directly to the video camera, the image is immediately sent to his system's hard disk. Billy can then print his image and add it to his insurance documentation and his database within minutes. Since these digital pictures also help Billy settle claims for his customers more quickly, he gets lots of business referrals.

Digital video cameras take digital imaging another step. You can videotape at your home, at work, or anywhere else and transmit those videos to others online or offline. Video conferences are not only possible but inexpensive. Video can be saved as Video for Windows or QuickTime files for use in office documents, Web transmission, or business multimedia projects.

Some digital video cameras can also be used as "frame grabbers"; they capture a single frame as a separate graphics file. The AOL Store's Digital Shop offers several digital video cameras and camera packages ranging in price from $99 to $349.

Connectix QuickCam

Here's a device that's very popular and inexpensive: Connectix's QuickCam VC is a small, color video camera that resembles a cue ball and plugs into your computer's parallel port (see figure 10.2). Since its 15-foot cord ties you close to your computer, QuickCam has some limitations. But you can have a lot of fun with QuickCam, using it for product demonstrations and video conferencing. Or you can use it to

128

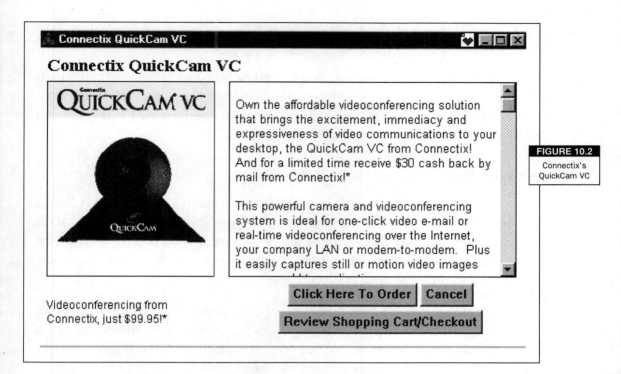

FIGURE 10.2
Connectix's
QuickCam VC

take single-frame digital pictures. QuickCam also offers a special AOL feature called QuickPICT, which lets you create e-mail messages with picture attachments to send to America Online and Internet users. You enable this feature when you install QuickCam for the first time.

Snappy

Snappy is an excellent and highly useful frame grabber that hooks up between your PC and a video camera. Considering that it uses a normal videocam for its input, the image quality is astonishing. Snappy can capture a single video screen at up to 1280 x 1024 resolution—the same level of quality as a megapixel digital camera. The Snappy Deluxe version includes several programs for simple image processing, including Adobe PhotoDeluxe, Gryphon Morph, and Kai's Power Goo Special Edition.

Each digital camera and frame grabber has its own unique features. Compare the digital cameras offered at the AOL Store. Take a little time to find exactly what you want. Use AOL's Computing channel to research your top candidates further, if necessary.

Producing Output

When you're talking about output, you can go in two directions: laser printers or color ink-jet printers. The market for both has never been better for consumers. Both kinds of printers are roughly comparable in price and performance at the low end and are more than adequate for small-office tasks.

Understanding Color Ink-Jet Printers

This is an area that's changing all the time. Ink-jet printers continue to get better, cheaper, and easier to use. A huge number of companies offer high-quality ink-jet printers, including Casio, Lexmark (see figure 10.3), and Epson. You can have a lot of creative fun if you buy the right printer for your imaging work—you can compare them in the Hardware Shop at the AOL Store.

The big buzzword in color ink-jets right now is "photo-quality." It simply indicates that the ink-jet in question prints a high-quality picture with such rich colors that it closely resembles a photograph. Ink-jet printer specs can be a bit confusing; the current state-of-the-art is probably defined by Epson, with stunning 1440 x 720 dpi

130

FIGURE 10.3
Lexmark 1000 Color JetPrinter

printing quality in its latest line of color printers. There are many others—so many, in fact, there's no way we could begin to describe them all.

One key thing to keep in mind about ink-jet printers is the type of paper they require for the best output. Many of the new color printers claim to produce highest-quality output even on plain paper, but special glossy paper works better for slicker print-outs. Naturally, no single printer maker uses the same kind of special paper as another, so you'll have to hunt around for the right stuff. Some of the latest printers will still produce their photo-quality images only on special glossy paper.

Ink-jets use a lot of ink. Typically, you can print 20 to 30 full-page color prints before replacing a color ink-jet cartridge. Most color printers use two separate cartridges: one for black ink, and another for full-color. The full-color cartridge usually contains three ink colors; cyan, magenta, and yellow, which are mixed with black to create the full range of colors in the printout.

If possible (in many cases it isn't), try to get a printer that uses four separate ink cartridges: cyan, yellow, magenta, and black. (Some new printers now use six colors for greater intensity. These are worth a look if you can find one!)

There are many alternatives to color ink-jet printers, including color laser, dye-sublimation, and monochrome or black-and-white laser printers (see figure 10.4). Color lasers are another rapidly growing market, but prices start at about $3,000, putting them out of reach of the average user. Hewlett-Packard (HP), GCC Technologies, Dataproducts, and Xante are the major competitors in this arena. Dye-sublimation printers tend to be very expensive and are suited for professional pre-press work. They generally provide the best possible image quality but at a very high price.

There's a huge selection of monochrome laser printers to choose from, with several levels of quality and speed at very reasonable prices. HP essentially dominates this market, with Lexmark and other companies competing. For overall small-office needs, we strongly recommend using a color ink-jet in conjunction with a black-and-white laser printer.

To learn more than we can fit into this book, go to the AOL Pictures area; there you can get help making the right purchase. The area includes numerous online magazines with experts on hand to advise you—for example, "Computer Life Online." AOL Pictures also lets you talk to photographic partners and experts from across the country. If you have a niggling problem with a device you've just bought, or need some pointers, this is a great place to go.

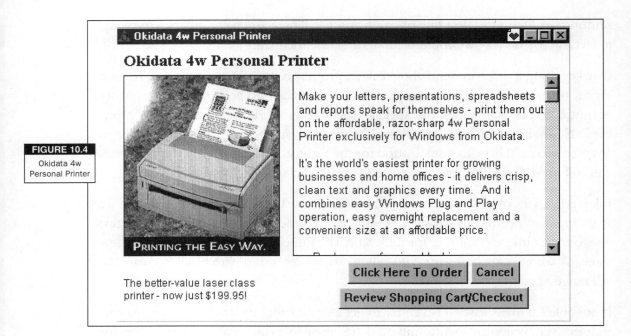

FIGURE 10.4

Okidata 4w
Personal Printer

Okidata 4w Personal Printer

Make your letters, presentations, spreadsheets and reports speak for themselves - print them out on the affordable, razor-sharp 4w Personal Printer exclusively for Windows from Okidata.

It's the world's easiest printer for growing businesses and home offices - it delivers crisp, clean text and graphics every time. And it combines easy Windows Plug and Play operation, easy overnight replacement and a convenient size at an affordable price.

PRINTING THE EASY WAY.

The better-value laser class printer - now just $199.95!

Click Here To Order   Cancel

Review Shopping Cart/Checkout

132

Using Photo Labs and PhotoCD

Up to now we've been talking a lot about how you can capture and produce your own images. We've also shown how these tools can help you pay a lot fewer visits to the local photo lab. When you use digital cameras and printers to create your own images, however, you may have difficulties preserving your work. Since a digital camera creates a computerized file of your image, your cherished images are vulnerable to the same problems as any computer file: misplacing them on your hard disk, accidentally deleting them, or even having a backup disk fail and losing the image file forever. Computers have occasional problems, no matter how careful you are. With a photograph and a negative, you'll never have these problems.

It is possible to have it both ways. If you don't mind the extra cost and time involved, you can use a regular camera to create digital files of your images with permanent, safe storage. You do this using the popular Kodak PhotoCD process; it turns photographic negatives into digital images and writes them onto a CD-ROM disk. With this strategy, you get excellent-quality images, but unfortunately, at a high cost: several dollars per image. The PhotoCD process is easy to use. Just be aware that your costs will increase.

Understanding Storage Options

Data storage and backup is an area where the user has a tremendous number of choices. An entire chapter could be written on this subject alone. If you have a relatively new computer, chances are you have a good-sized hard disk installed. Unfortunately, Windows applications and the files they create can be huge, gobbling up disk space in carload lots. That's especially the case with image and graphics files. Fortunately, it's easy to find solutions.

It all boils down to one term: removable drives. In that simple term lies a multitude of possibilities for successful data management. A removable drive is a disk-based device that you can read from and write information to, then remove when you're finished. One increasingly popular and affordable choice is a writable CD-ROM drive.

Writable CD-ROMs, also called CD-Rs, offer the powerful advantage of producing disks that can be read by any system with a CD-ROM drive. Their biggest disadvantage is that once you write to a CD-R disc, you cannot write to it again. It's a write-once-read-many medium. Another variant, called CD-RW, is a bit more expensive but allows basically unlimited writes to the same disk. This is usually the best option.

Another great option is a high-capacity drive such as the Iomega Jaz or SyQuest SyJet. Both offer gigabyte capacities (Jaz provides 1 GB or 2 GB, while the SyJet provides 1.5 GB) per disk, and you can buy as many disks as you want. Iomega's very popular Zip drive is a highly useful tool. (Another popular manufacturer of storage devices is Imation.) It's cheap, and the odds are that you already have one sitting on your desk.

Finally, you can also buy a second or larger hard drive for your system and have a technician install it for you. A typical PC-type hard drive can hold as much as 8 GB of data, and bigger ones yet are on the way. Even better, they're cheap. Multi-gigabyte hard disks are standard in the PC world, and even the smallest ones commonly sold now contain about 2 GB and sell for well under $200.

Many other options exist, such as tape and optical drives, but tape is best used as a backup tool for your entire system (which is highly recommended), while high-capacity optical drives are far too expensive for the average user. If you become a serious graphics user, an optical drive is something to think about, but for the applica-

133

tions described here, their price-performance ratio is nowhere near as good as the other devices in this section.

Understanding Video Cards

Here's another arena where PC users can get lost in the details. Your PC's video card is the foundation for your imaging work. High-speed video cards are the rule in almost every new PC sold today. A lot of exciting technology goes into the process of making your computer crank out the fastest graphics possible; none of that will be described in any detail here.

Just be assured that the products are generally better than ever, cheaper than ever, and more sophisticated yet easier to use than ever before. Among the best companies making video cards are Number Nine, ATI, Diamond, STB, Hercules, and Matrox. The AOL Store (keyword: **AOL Store**) offers many cards from these makers—so many they can't all be named here. Not only that: what is state-of-the-art in the video card arena changes so fast, the hottest card of six months ago is today's remainder item.

With Windows 95, it's easy to replace your existing video card with the newest model, because every manufacturer makes their cards "plug and play" and usually provides good software drivers to make sure they work with your system. Best of all, even the hottest cards usually cost $200 or less. If your system needs a booster shot, consider buying a new video card instead of replacing the whole system. AOL can help you research video cards so you can make an informed buying decision.

Memory

Imaging applications require a lot of memory. You'll need 16 megabytes of RAM at a minimum; 32 megabytes is recommended. Fortunately, upgrading your system's memory is one of the simplest upgrades you can undertake. The AOL Store's Hardware Shop includes a complete selection of memory modules.

11

THE POWER OF GRAPHICS SOFTWARE

Right about now you might feel ready to take some graphics software for a spin. Would you like to spruce up some photographs or add some special effects? Get an imaging program. Do you enjoy creating your own illustrations or wish you could draw? Try a drawing program. You can also create professional-looking newsletters, brochures, and other pieces with a wordprocessing or desktop publishing program. If you would like building exciting presentations and animations with images and audio, try out some of the great multimedia and presentation programs out there. Or try them all, if you want.

Is it expensive? Not necessarily. It depends on what you want to do with your digital pictures. Some of the higher-end programs are expensive. Other programs cost hardly anything at all, and you can try them before you buy them. To download lots of cool shareware goodies, enter the keyword **Computing** and visit the Computing channel. There you'll find tips, resources, and downloadable software galore—along with a fun grabbag of multimedia files created by your fellow AOL members.

So dive in and get creative. Turn ordinary pictures into impressionist paintings. Create your own drawings and designs. Design your own holiday cards and brochures. Or use your digital pictures in exciting, animated presentations with sound. This chapter tells you about different types of graphics programs, what you can do with them, and how to get them.

Image Programs

Pictures revive special memories. But they don't always look quite the way we'd like them to. You'd like to share the pictures you took of your newborn daughter. But your pictures of little Kaitlin look more like *Rosemary's Baby* than *your* baby. Her pretty blue eyes turned red when the camera flash went off. Does this mean you can't take pictures of Kaitlin indoors? What about that photo you took of your sister last year? She looks great—if only you could cut her ex-husband out of the picture. A favorite old photograph of Grandma and Grandpa on their wedding day is crumbling around the edges. You'd like to repair it. Or maybe you'd simply like to convert your TIF photographs to JPEGs so you can use them in your Web page.

So why do Sarah's pictures always look perfect? She does all kinds of neat things with digital pictures, and has even bought a color printer. She turns in polished reports and proposals at work. Her friends, family, and coworkers love getting her homemade mini-photo album booklets as gifts. Sarah's calendars sell like crazy at school and church fund-raisers. Her neighbors, friends, and colleagues always say, "I never knew you were a photographer—your pictures always come out perfectly." Sarah laughs and says, "I'm no photographer." But nobody believes her. Is Sarah just being modest? No. She doesn't know how to use a camera any better than you do. But she does know how to use her image software.

With a good imaging program you can:

- **Crop pictures.** Say good-bye to ex-boyfriends and girlfriends, tourists who wander into the frame, unsightly smokestacks, your thumb, and other unwanted parts of your pictures.

- **Touch up problem areas.** Get rid of red-eye and restore people's eyes to their normal color. And while you're at it, erase those skin blemishes and coffee stains.

- **Convert images to different formats.** Use the same picture for your printed pieces, Web page, and e-mail message attachments. You can convert your digital pictures to any format you need.

- **Resize pictures.** Make your pictures smaller or larger.

- **Adjust brightness, contrast, and color.** Bring dark, blurry pictures into focus. Or add a little color to washed-out-looking photographs.

- **Add special effects.** Turn ordinary photographs into extraordinary ones with a variety of special effects. You can make your pictures looks like museum-quality paintings, old-fashioned sepia-tone photographs, and more.

- **Doctor your photographs.** Would you like to repair damaged pictures, remove objects without a trace, or blend different photographs together seamlessly? With some time, effort, and a willingness to learn, you and your image program can work miracles.

- **Have fun.** With image programs, you can mix and match parts of your images with hilarious results. Take a picture of Newt Gingrich's head and put it on Hillary Clinton's body. Make wild and crazy photo collages.

So how do you get started? First, find the right image software program. We'll tell you how to use AOL to find the software, and how to use AOL's own built-in image program, the Picture Gallery. Then you can read about touching-up images and adding special effects in chapters 12 and 13.

What's an Image Program?

You may not realize it, but you already know about image programs—you've even used one or two. AOL's built-in Picture Gallery image editing window, shown in figure 11.1, is a simple image program. So is the Paint program that comes with Windows. Image programs have tools for editing and saving your images.

For instance, you can adjust brightness and contrast levels, or crop your pictures. Image programs represent digital pictures as *bitmaps*, tiny dots of color that combine to form an image. Each one of those dots is called a *pixel*, the smallest unit of measurement on your computer screen. When you make changes to your picture, the program applies your changes to each pixel. For example, if you click on the Picture Gallery's Brighten button to make your image lighter, the program makes each pixel lighter.

You can do a lot with your free image programs. The Picture Gallery image editing window has tools for things like cropping and rotating images and adjusting the brightness and contrast. (Chapter 2 explains the Picture Gallery image editing win-

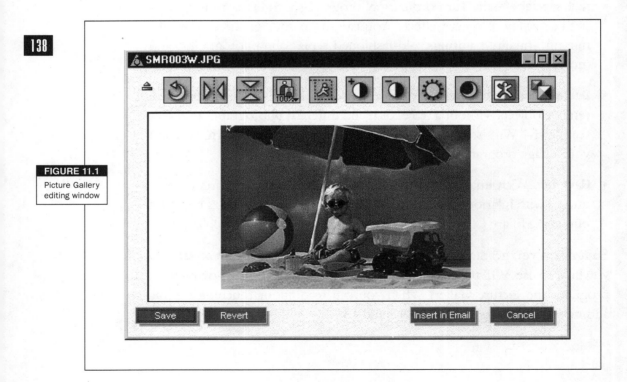

FIGURE 11.1
Picture Gallery editing window

138

dow's tools in greater detail.) The Windows Paint program has painting and drawing tools, an eraser, and a text tool so you can touch up images pixel by pixel, add text, erase parts of the image, draw, and fill in shapes. However, these tools have their limitations. You can't convert an image to a different file format with the Picture Gallery image editing window, nor can you paint or add text. Paint can only open and save BMP and PCX files, and lacks the Picture Gallery's image editing tools.

Sure, you can try using both Paint and the Picture Gallery to get your image to look the way you want it. But when you are ready for more, you need a more powerful image program, one that has a wide range of editing and special-effects tools, and that can open and convert all kinds of images—including JPEGs, GIFs, BMPs, PCXs, and TIFs. In most programs you can draw lines and shapes, convert images, add text, and apply special effects. If the sky looks too cloudy, you can make it bluer. You can select the beach ball and put it in the dump truck. Or you can crop out everything except the child, and make the umbrella disappear by painting it the same color as the sky.

Image programs can be costly because they do a lot of things. But you don't have to break the bank. Listed below are some moderately priced popular image programs.

- **PaintShop Pro** Priced at about $130 and packed with features, Jasc Software's PaintShop Pro is the best deal in town. It does just about everything the more expensive programs do for a fraction of the price. Unless you plan on becoming a graphic designer or prepress specialist, PaintShop Pro has everything you need. You can download text.

- **ThumbsPlus** Maybe you don't plan on touching up your digital pictures much, and think the Picture Gallery and Paint will do just fine, thank you. But you'd sure like to find a tool that can convert images and help you catalog them. If this sounds like you, try Cerious Software's ThumbsPlus. It costs about $70 and can open and convert most types of files. In addition, it makes it easy to keep track of your digital pictures, as chapter 14 explains in greater detail.

- **PhotoPaint** If you also need a drawing and presentation program, consider purchasing the Corel Graphics Suite. It comes with everything but

139

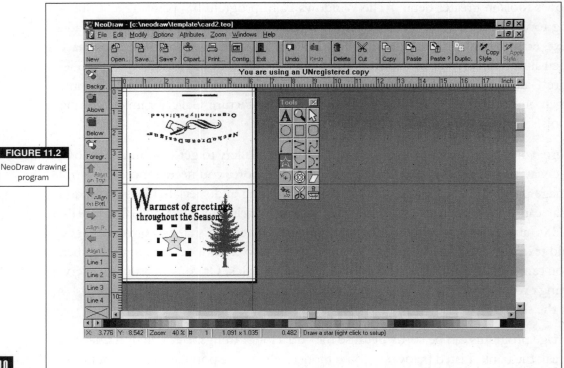

the kitchen sink—including Corel's PhotoPaint image program—for about $500. This is a bargain if you need a variety of graphics software. You can't download the Corel Graphics Suite—you have to buy it in a store.

- **PhotoShop** Graphics and imaging professionals swear by Adobe's Photo-Shop and gladly fork over about $500 for it. If you plan on getting serious about working with images, or plan to pursue it professionally, then you probably should too. Otherwise, you'll do just fine with PaintShop Pro or ThumbsPlus.

So, do you want to get started? Download PaintShop Pro and try it out right now. Chapter 12 covers the basics—such as cropping, removing red-eye, and converting images. Chapter 13 goes on to explain advanced imaging techniques and special effects.

Drawing Programs

John and his kids are artists. They're always drawing and designing things—holiday and greeting cards, posters for Jenny's upcoming Girl Scout cookie sale, flyers for Tom's fledgling snow-shoveling business. Since they enjoy creating their own illustrations and designs, they use a drawing program. A drawing program is sort of like a paint program. Some of the tools even look the same. But there's an important difference. Drawing programs represent images as *vectors,* not bitmaps. Vector programs define lines, shapes, and objects mathematically instead of by pixels. Even the toolbar buttons look like diagrams from your geometry textbook.

Drawing programs give you greater control over all the lines, shapes, and objects you create. If you make a bitmap image smaller or larger, the image may get blurry. Vector graphics stay crisp and clear no matter how much you resize them. Because they offer this level of precision, drawing programs are ideal for creating illustrations and logos, as well as arranging and positioning graphics and text for cards, flyers, simple brochures, and more.

Because drawing programs are so complex, they can be expensive. Programs like Adobe Illustrator and Macromedia Freehand cost around $600 and are popular among graphic designers and illustrators. A lot of people also use Corel Draw, which comes with the Corel Graphics Suite mentioned in the "Image Programs" section of this chapter. If you're not ready to dive in with both feet yet, you can try NeoSoft's NeoDraw, as shown in figure 11.2. It costs about $40, is easy to use, and has lots of great features. Look for it at the Computer channel (keyword: **Computers**).

Desktop Publishing

Matt works as an administrative assistant for a marketing company. Of course, he'd rather be doing something more creative, but he just got out of school and has to work his way up. When he became an AOL member and started getting into digital pictures, he saw an opportunity. Matt noticed that many people on the forums and chat groups he visits create newsletters for their businesses. He thought it might be a good idea for his company to have a newsletter too. He bought Microsoft Publisher, created a sample newsletter, and showed it to his boss. She was impressed and added a monthly newsletter to Matt's job description. Matt's coworkers and the

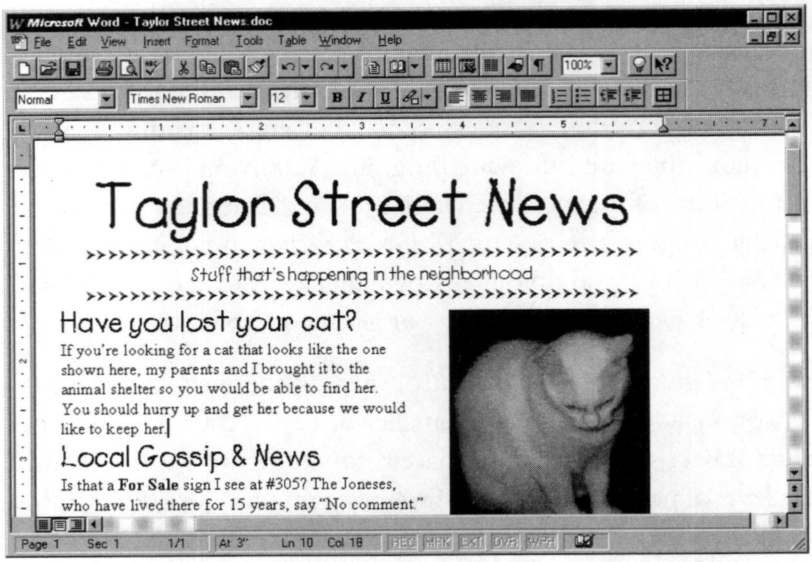

FIGURE 11.3
A newsletter in Microsoft Word

company's clients like the new publication. Plus, he now gets to network with clients and people all over the company while preparing his articles.

If you use your digital pictures in reports, proposals, and other complex documents, a desktop publishing program can help. Desktop publishing programs are sort of a cross between your word processor and a drawing program. Like word processors, they have lots of editing features so you can work with text. Yet, like drawing programs, desktop publishing software makes it easy to position and arrange text and graphic elements. QuarkXpress and Adobe PageMaker are the most popular desktop publishing applications. Yet their price tags are often beyond the reach of people who don't do desktop publishing and graphic design for a living. QuarkXpress costs over $900. PageMaker costs about $500.

Fortunately, you have more affordable options for experimenting with digital pictures and creating publications. For many people, good word processing software does the trick. Microsoft Word and Corel WordPerfect both include features for working with text and images. Although you lose some flexibility, word processing programs still let you create simple, professional-looking layouts like the one shown in figure 11.3. Microsoft Publisher is also a good desktop publishing program. It comes with lots of ready-to-use templates and clip art, and costs less than $200. For more information about Adobe PageMaker, visit Adobe's Web site at keyword **Adobe**. To learn more about Microsoft Publisher, use keyword **Microsoft**.

Presentations

How many times have your kids wound up in situations like Shelley's? She had to deliver an oral report on Thomas Jefferson to her fifth-grade class. She wasn't worried about the research—she loves history and had already done all of her research and written the report. But she felt really nervous about talking in front of everyone. Fortunately, there's a computer in her classroom. Her teacher suggested that maybe turning her report into a computer presentation would make her feel less shy.

Shelley went home, logged on to AOL, and searched the Computer channel for a user-friendly slide show program (see figure 11.4). She found a shareware program by PC WholeWare called Slim Show that could create presentations, and she

FIGURE 11.4
A shareware slide show program

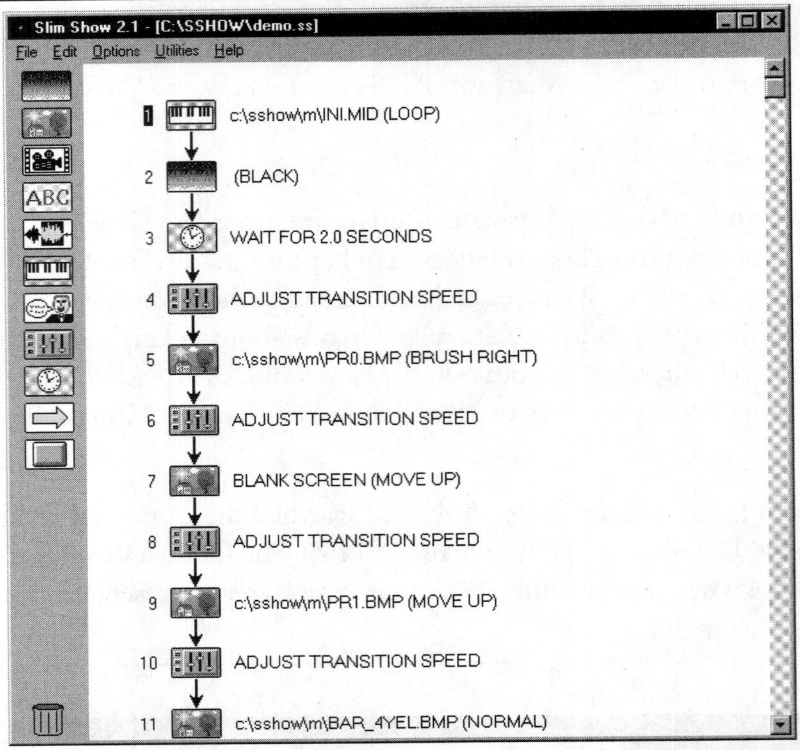

FIGURE 11.5

Slim Show presentation

decided to try it out. She then searched AOL and the Internet for pictures of Jefferson, the signing of the Declaration of Independence, Jefferson's estate at Monticello, and other historical figures from Jefferson's time. After her father helped her to download about 30 photos, she was ready to begin creating her presentation.

Shelley installed the program—which lets her try it for a few weeks before she has to persuade her parents to pay for it—then began figuring out how to build her presentation. Like most slide show programs, Slim Show consists of a series of frames, as shown in figure 11.5. Each frame moves the presentation forward. Slim Show also has tools for adding images, text, audio, and special effects to each frame.

Within a few hours, Shelley was happy with her presentation. The next morning she woke up early, and uploaded them so she could download on the computer at school. She was so excited about her presentation she forgot to be shy. Her classmates all wanted to know how she did it so they could make their reports more interesting too.

Would you like to impress your friends, family, classmates, or colleagues with some multimedia? You can create exciting presentations with animated images and sound. Best of all, the software you need is inexpensive—or free. Visit the Computer channel and try out Slim Show. If you have Microsoft Office installed at home, work, or school, you can also check out PowerPoint. PowerPoint is easy to use and helps you create professional-looking multimedia presentations with digital pictures, audio, video, and special effects. The PowerPoint Viewer even lets you display presentations to people who don't have the program.

145

12

TOUCHING UP AND IMPROVING PICTURES

Would you like to spruce up your digital pictures? Whether you're a small business owner, a professional photographer going digital, or just someone who wants to make the most of your photographs, you can make your so-so pictures shine, or make the good ones even better. All it takes is a good image program like Corel Photopaint, or Adobe Photoshop, and a little insider knowledge. You can order Photopaint from Corel's Web site at the AOL Store or find out more about PhotoShop by going to keyword **Adobe**. So what would you like to do? Remove red-eye? Get your pictures ready for your Web page? Convert images to a different file

TIPS FOR SCANNING IMAGES

It's better to scan an image correctly to begin with than to have to make major touchups later or scan the whole thing over. The following tips will help you scan with better results.

- **Scan at 300 dpi.** You can always reduce an image's resolution, but you can't increase it. Scanning your image at 300 dpi! gives you more flexibility.

- **Prescan the image.** Many scanner software programs, including PhotoShop LE, let you prescan. This lets you preview the image and adjust the scanner settings before doing the final scan.

- **Orient the image.** Scanners will often flip-flop your image. Make sure the picture is placed correctly on the scanner.

- **Make sure the image is lying straight.** You'd be surprised how often we forget to do this.

148

format? Make your own enlargements and wallet-sized photos to send to friends and relatives? This chapter gives you the low down. It tells you about some easy ways to improve and touch up your pictures. You don't know what the word "analog" means? Read on! This chapter gets you well on your way toward becoming a digital-imaging expert. Chapter 13 then reveals some graphic designers' and imaging professionals' secrets for doctoring photos and adding special effects.

Digital and Analog Pictures— What's the Difference?

You already know what digital pictures are. You've been playing with them throughout the book. They're regular pictures that have been converted to a format that your computer understands. You get them onto your computer with scanners, a digital camera, or a camcorder. These products are explained in chapter 10. Or you can take a roll of film to the developing lab and have them put your pictures on a CD-ROM or disk. Digital pictures are stored on your hard drive, in your digital camera, on a CD-ROM, or other external storage device (for more about storing and archiving pictures, see chapter 15).

So what's an *analog* picture? It's the "real" thing—a picture you can hold in your hand. Scanners turn analog pictures into digital pictures. When you take pictures with a digital camera or camcorder and transfer them to your computer, you never see the analog picture—unless you print it out. A printer *outputs* your pictures—in other words, it converts your digital picture into an analog picture you can put in a frame or mail to your friends via the U.S. Postal Service.

Now, your computer might be smart. But it still doesn't "see" things the same way a human being does. When you scan a photograph, the digital conversion doesn't look exactly like the analog version. When you print out the picture you scanned, it doesn't look exactly like either the original *or* what you see on your computer screen.

Most of the time, this doesn't matter. Your digital pictures and your printouts may look a little different, but you'll barely be able to tell the difference. But if you understand how digital pictures work and how they compare with analog pictures, you'll be able to do more with them.

The Importance of Resolution

We've already mentioned *resolution* in chapter 10. With computers, there's print resolution and image resolution. Print resolution is measured in *dpi*—dots per inch. The more dots a printer can print per inch, the more detail you get. Most people have printers that can produce pages with 300 or 600 dpi. And, 300 dpi is perfectly fine for printing out good-quality text and images. Computer resolution is measured in *pixels,* short for "picture elements." Pixels are the tiny dots that, all together, form your image. Higher resolution means more detail and higher image quality. But higher-resolution images take up more disk space. Lower resolution means less detail and lower image quality. But low-resolution images take up a lot less disk space. Since image programs were originally designed to help people touch up and print images, they refer to image resolution as dpi. But keep in mind that we're dealing with pixels here.

Now, here's where things can get a little confusing. Your computer screen can only display images at 96 dpi. A 96 dpi image looks fine on your computer screen. It's ideal for images that people will only see on a computer. If you're using images on a Web page, or in a multimedia or presentation program, you should use 96 dpi images to save disk space. If you plan on printing an image, you'll need to use 300 dpi images to get decent image quality (some people prefer 600 dpi images or higher, but these hog up disk space and take forever to print). The 300 dpi picture won't look any better than a 96 dpi picture when you view it on your computer screen. But the difference will be obvious if you print it out.

How Imaging Programs Display Pictures

So, if a computer can't display resolutions higher than 96 dpi, what happens if you open a 300 dpi picture in your image program? It looks bigger. Figure 12.1 shows the same picture at 96 dpi and 300 dpi. Both images have the same height and width measurements. But the 300 dpi one looks much bigger. If you print the two images, the printouts will both be the same size. However, the 300 dpi printout will look great and the 96 dpi picture will probably look terrible. When you import the image into a word processing or desktop publishing program, the image appears at its printing size. The good imaging programs all have options for adjusting an image's horizontal and vertical resolution (though the horizontal and vertical numbers should both be the same). Adjusting the resolution or resizing the image is also sometimes called "resampling" the image.

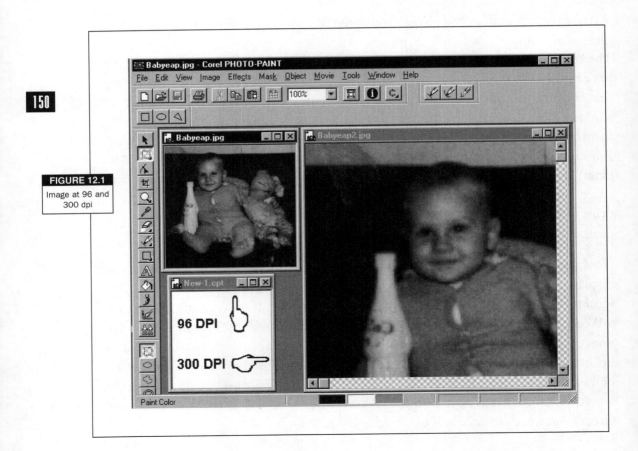

FIGURE 12.1

Image at 96 and 300 dpi

How Computers Handle Colors

Computers view colors as combinations of red, green, and blue (RGB), with white and black to lighten or darken them. Image programs give you several ways to choose colors. They all offer options similar to the ones shown in Corel PhotoPaint's dialogue box, as shown in figure 12.2. You can either select a color from a palette (little squares of color), pick a custom color by moving a color slider up and down, or (if you know a lot about computers and colors) select a color mode (the one shown is RGB) and enter numerical values. In most situations, entering numerical values isn't necessary to pick the right color. All image programs have similar systems for picking and displaying colors.

How Printers Handle Colors

Printers, on the other hand, handle colors as combinations of cyan (an intense light blue), magenta, yellow, and black. For some reason, this is called CMYK instead of

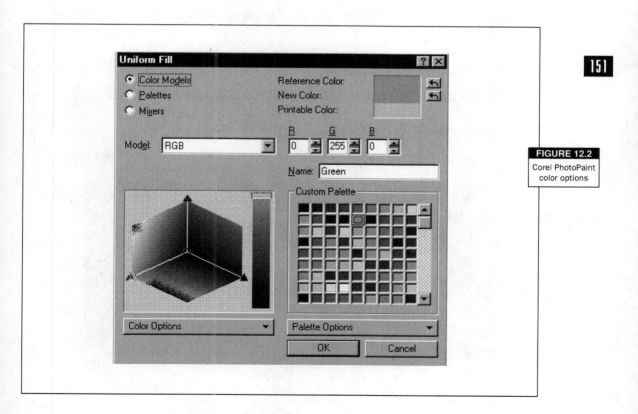

FIGURE 12.2

Corel PhotoPaint color options

CMYB. Image programs try to help people who want the colors on their computer screen to match their printer output. They offer a CMYK color mode that comes fairly close to displaying colors as they will appear when you print out the image. However, the colors don't always match perfectly. Put two or three graphic designers in a room together, and they'll talk about printing and color issues for hours. Fortunately, the rest of us seldom need to worry about that. We don't produce glossy magazines with millions of dollars' worth of ads that have to look absolutely perfect. We just want to have fun, improve our business materials and school reports, and send a birthday card to Grandma.

Photo Rx 101: The Basics

You'd like to start making your pictures look good, right? But first, let's take a quick look at pixels. When you become a digital pictures insider, you'll wind up looking at pixels a lot. If you zoom in really close, as shown in figure 12.3, you'll see the individual pixels that make up the image. Zooming in makes pictures look a little

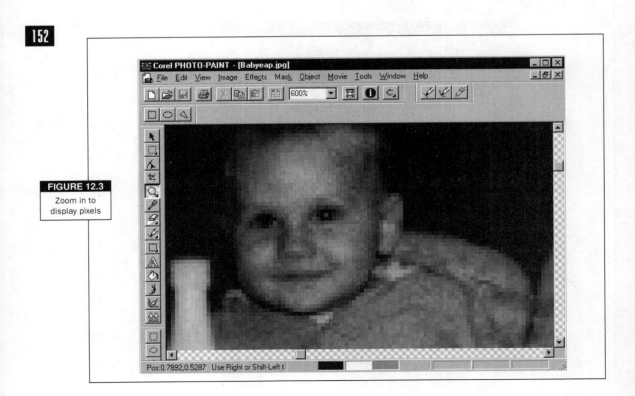

FIGURE 12.3

Zoom in to display pixels

strange and computerized, but don't worry. When you zoom out, the picture looks normal again. Touching up pictures means adjusting pixel colors. When you adjust a picture's brightness, the image program makes all the pixels lighter. Or you can select areas of the picture with the masking tools and change all the pixels within that area. Finally, you can use the paintbrush tool to recolor smaller numbers of pixels.

Don't be scared. It's easy once you get the hang of it. This chapter shows examples created in Corel PhotoPaint. But PaintShop Pro and Adobe Photo-Shop also provide these capabilities. Think of yourself as an artist, and the image program as your paintbox full of tools for just about anything you need to do. The following sections tell you how to crop pictures, remove red-eye, and more—quickly and easily. When you finish, nobody will be able to tell what was done. Instead, your friends, family, and colleagues will marvel at your photographic abilities. Only you can decide whether to tell the truth, or keep this as our little secret.

When you open your image program, look for the following buttons on the toolbar:

- **Selection.** This selects masked objects and moves or resizes them.

- **Masking.** With this group of tools, you can select a group of pixels to copy, paste, or change. You can draw a circular mask, a rectangular mask, or use the lasso masking tool to draw an area free-hand style. There is also a magic wand. When you click an area of the image, the wand masks all contiguous areas that are the same color as the selected area.

WHAT'S ANTI-ALIASING?

No, anti-aliasing doesn't mean forcing underworld spies to go only by their real names. It's a process that blurs the edges when you paint, apply special effects to masked areas, enter text, or fill in shapes. This enables new elements to blend in with the picture more seamlessly. If you need more precision, you can turn anti-aliasing off in the image program's settings.

- **Eyedropper.** Click the eyedropper on a color to choose a color for your paintbrush. You can select colors from the image or from the color palette. All image programs come with a color palette.

- **Zoom tool.** Click on the magnifying glass to quickly zoom in on an area of your picture. Image programs also offer menu options for zooming back out.

- **Cropping tool.** Use the cropping tool to select part of an image and discard the remainder.

- **Paintbrush tool.** Use the paintbrush tool to draw on an image or touch up colors pixel by pixel. You can adjust the size and texture of the paintbrush.

- **Fill tool.** This fills in masked areas with a selected color or pattern.

- **Text tool.** Use this to enter text on your picture. You can choose fonts, styles, and colors for your text.

- **Eraser.** This erases an area of the image.

Image programs also offer a wide variety of other tools. While we can't cover them all in this book, we'll get you up and running so you can make the most of your digital pictures now and learn more later. In addition, image programs let you choose a background, or canvascolor, and a foreground color. The foreground color appears when you use the paintbrush or fill tool. The background color appears when you erase or cut parts of an image.

Viewing and Converting Pictures

Your uncle Fred e-mails you and says he'd love to look at that photo you sent of the kids, but unfortunately, he can't open your TIF file. Tsk, tsk. If he had signed up with AOL, he would have been able to view it in the Picture Gallery. What can you do? Convert it to a PCX or BMP so Uncle Fred can open the image in the Paint program that comes with his Windows system. Now you'd like to add the same picture to your Web page. But Web browsers can only display GIFs and JPEGs. No problem.

With image programs, viewing and converting pictures is easy. You simply open and save them the way you would with any program. Select the Open command from the File menu, then look for your picture in the dialogue box. When the picture appears in the application window, select Save As from the File menu and select a new file format.

This is also a good place to mention the difference between RGB color and *indexed color* modes. In order to save an image to the GIF format, you must first convert it to indexed color mode. Image programs all have options for doing that. RGB color images can run the full gamut of the millions of colors available on your computer. Indexed color images are limited to the 256 standard system palette colors. Why would anyone want images with a limited number of colors? Line art and logos display more boldly in indexed color mode. You can also do fun things with GIF files on your Web pages that you can't do with other types of images—such as create GIF animations and eliminate the image's background color so it displays seamlessly against the Web page's background.

Reducing and Enlarging Pictures

When we said you can start your own digital pictures lab, back in chapter 10, we weren't kidding. You can enlarge and reduce pictures to any size you want (though enlarged images may distort if you make them *too* large). So go ahead. Print out an 8 x 10 glossy for Mom and Dad, and some wallet-sized photos for your other relatives. All digital imaging programs have a dialogue box for resizing images. Some of them call it "resampling" an image. Don't get confused between changing a picture's size (horizontal and vertical dimensions) and changing an image's resolution. These options generally appear in the same dialogue box. Also keep in mind that you should resize your images proportionally. If you make Aunt Sally taller, but not wider, people may wonder if she tried the latest fad diet! Image programs offer options for automatically resizing pictures proportionally.

Adjusting Brightness and Contrast

Image programs also have brightness and contrast controls, as shown in figure 12.4. These let you shed a whole new light on dark, indistinct photographs, or lend substance to those that look washed out. To adjust brightness and contrast, select the option from the menu, then simply move the sliders back and forth until the image appears the way you want. Image programs also let you preview the image

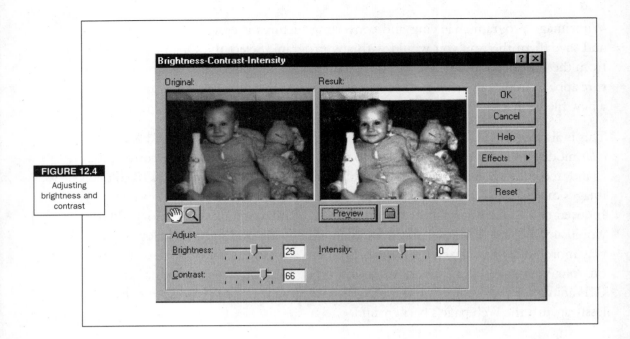

FIGURE 12.4

Adjusting
brightness and
contrast

with the brightness or contrast adjusted before you apply it to the file. But remember, if you don't like something you've just done, you can press the CTRL+Z key combination to undo it.

Removing Red-Eye

We've all had this problem. You and your friends go to a party together and you take a great picture of everyone. But of course, somebody always winds up with red, glowing eyes because of the flash. This looks particularly disturbing in pictures of babies and young children. Some of us may even remember our parents attacking our pictures with black magic marker to get the red out of our eyes. Which of course made things even worse (unless you enjoy looking like a cartoon character).

Now you can say good-bye to red-eye once and for all. Image programs give you the tools you need to retouch pictures unobtrusively. You don't need to be an expert. If you can draw a few dots, you can replace red with your friend's normal eye color.

First, click the zoom tool over the eyes to get a closer look. You'll find that in many cases, you can still see parts of your friend's real eye color. Click the eyedropper on the real color of your friend's eyes. Or display the color palettes and color adjustment tools and pick the closest color. Then take your paintbrush and click it on all the red parts to paint over them. And remember to first check your brush size before trying this. To do detailed touchups like this, the brush should only be one pixel wide. Now, zoom back out. There. Doesn't that look better?

Once you get good at getting rid of red-eye, you can put your new skills to good use. For example, if a friend had a blemish on her skin that day, be nice and touch it up for her. Simply click the eyedropper on an area of skin near the blemish (but not on it) to match the skin color, then use the paintbrush to zap it away.

Cropping Pictures

Your sister just broke up with her boyfriend. That's too bad, because your only recent picture of her also has him in it. Now she says you can't use that picture on your Web page anymore. How can you get rid of this guy? With digital pictures, it's

FIGURE 12.5

Cropping a picture

easy. A few snips with the cropping tool, and he's gone! Figure 12.5 shows how to crop someone out of a photo, add some finishing touches, and give your picture a whole new lease on life. First, select the cropping tool and draw a square around the area you want to keep. Everything outside the edges gets cut out. Since the (then) loving couple was standing close together, we can only keep your sister's head in the picture. So, you wind up with a picture that still has a little bit of the ex's hair in it (top right). You can use your paintbrush or fill tool to get rid of that. And finally, you have a picture of your sister you can keep (bottom right). And if they get back together, you still have the original picture. Pretty slick, huh?

Some Advanced Techniques

One of the best things about digital imaging is that even when life isn't picture perfect, you can make your pictures look that way. Did slightly overcast weather cloud your vacation at the shore? Make the sky a little bluer. Does a sunburn make your nose glow like Rudolph the Red-Nosed Reindeer's? Touch it up so it matches the rest of your skin. You can even rotate your picture, or part of your picture, just for fun.

Masking

Masking is one of the main secrets to digital imaging. The masking tools let you draw areas around your images to select them. You can define a circular mask by using the circle mask tool, or use the rectangle mask tool to define a square or rectangular mask. The lasso tool lets you draw around an area freehand, or you can use the magic wand tool to select an area of color. Once you mask an area, you can cut or copy it and paste it somewhere else, apply a special effect, or adjust the area's colors. Imaging programs apply your changes only to the masked area. If you don't mask an area and then apply a special effect (chapter 13 tells you about special effects you can add to your pictures), or adjust the colors, contrast, or brightness, the changes are applied to the entire image.

Masking can take a little time to get the hang of, so be patient. But once you get good at it, you can do all kinds of fun things, like compositing pictures, removing parts of the picture without a trace, doctoring scans of damaged photographs, and making your pictures look like paintings.

Color Correction

With image programs, you can adjust colors in your pictures, or masked areas within your pictures. For example, let's say you wish the sky looked more blue. That's easy. Image programs all provide settings for hue, saturation, and brightness levels (HSB). You can adjust these levels by moving a slider back and forth and previewing your image until you get the right color.

The Hue setting determines the color—such as whether the picture or masked area is gray, purple, or blue. The Saturation setting determines the intensity of the color. Since making the sky a brilliant turquoise blue would look unnatural, you may prefer to go with a more washed-out (less-saturated) shade of blue. The Brightness set-

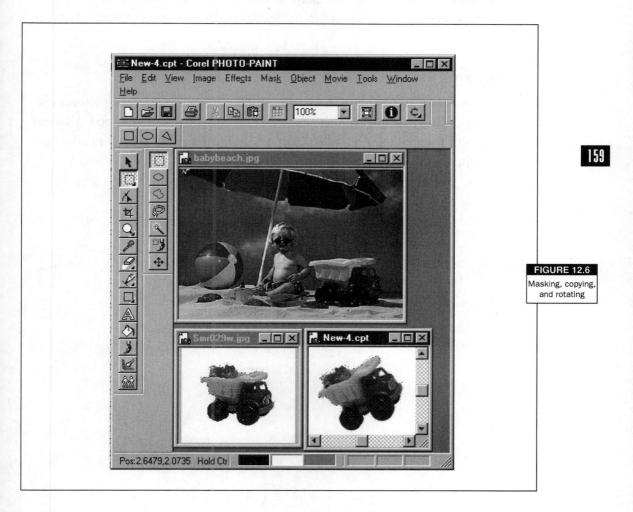

FIGURE 12.6

Masking, copying, and rotating

ting determines how light or dark the color is. Don't forget to select your sky with the magic wand tool or by drawing around it with the lasso tool. Otherwise, all the colors in your picture will change.

Copying, Pasting, Distorting, and Rotating Image Areas

Your digital image software does more for you when you know how to mask areas, then copy, paste, distort, and rotate them. Take figure 12.6, for example. If you use the lasso tool to draw an area around the dump truck, you can copy and paste it into a new picture. You can also rotate the dump truck and use it to add interest to your desktop publishing or Web page design. Image programs also let you stretch selected areas, flip them horizontally or vertically, rotate them, and more. When you pick a tool, a selection box appears so you can make changes by dragging the box's handles or moving the box.

Blurring and Sharpening

Your image program also lets you sharpen and blur images. Sharpening pictures creates an effect similar to increasing the contrast: images look more defined. You can also use the blur tool to create a soft-focus effect. Some programs let you preview the amount of blurring.

13

ADVANCED IMAGING AND SPECIAL EFFECTS

The touchups described in chapter 12 can do wonders for your digital pictures. Once you've mastered the basics, you can take digital imaging to a whole new level. Would you like to get rid of a crack running down the center of a favorite turn-of-the-century photo? How about morphing two images into one? And don't forget about creating backgrounds, buttons, and special text effects you can use in multimedia slide shows or on your Web pages. With a little time and some good imaging software, you can turn your digital pictures into unique works of art.

TIPS FOR BETTER PICTURES

While every insider should know how to touch up, improve, and add artistic effects to digital pictures, you can save a lot of time by taking good photographs to begin with. You already know the basics—we've included photography pointers throughout the book. However, here's a recap.

- **Use your zoom lens.** Close-ups grab more attention and make your subject look more interesting. This especially holds true when taking pictures of people. Look at professional photographs and advertisements in magazines. They often feature close-ups because most people enjoy looking at faces.
- **Capture candid moments of people in motion.** Action shots—of people baking, hugging, running, raking leaves, or playing, for example—make the best photographs. This means you shouldn't be afraid to get unusual shots and use up rolls of film. Look at any professional photographer's contact sheets and you'll see all the ho-hum shots they had to take in order to get those two or three amazing ones.
- **Use the right film speed.** ASA 100 film works best for pictures taken in broad daylight, while ASA 400 to 1000 film is ideal for pictures taken indoors or at night. With ASA 1000 film and a slower shutter speed, you can often take indoor pictures without a flash, if there's a little light coming from somewhere. This can help you avoid the washed-out look and red, glowing eyes caused by a flash. Keep in mind that ASA 100 film only works well in daylight or with a flash, and 1000 film only works well at night. If you want a little more flexibility to take pictures wherever and whenever you want, use ASA 200 or 400 film.
- **Take advantage of today's technologies.** Are you taking a vacation to the Grand Canyon? Or driving through the desert? Do you have a family reunion coming up and need to cram about 50 people into a single picture? Then use panoramic film to get the widest pictures. To get a smooth picture when filming high-speed events (like a soccer game) or capture movies in old-fashioned sepia tones, check to see if your video camera has special settings.
- **Use light and shadow.** Artists call this technique "chiaroscuro." When composing your photographs, make sure the scene has plenty of contrast between light and dark areas. This adds visual interest to your photographs. But too bright light can make your picture look washed out and too dim light can make it look dark and indistinct. If the light isn't right, try moving your subject to a brighter or darker location, or take the picture at a different time of day.
- **Pay attention to color.** If you plan on taking a family portrait, think about the colors everyone looks best in and advise them to wear these colors. Whether shooting a picture of an object or scene, consider color contrast. Bright yellow flowers may not show up well against a beige or yellow house, while pink, blue, or purple ones should contrast beautifully. A picture of the gray Manhattan skyline may not look so impressive on a gray, cloudy day. Majestic blue mountains fading into a twilit sky may create an ethereal effect, but the mountains will not be well defined.
- **Notice how objects are arranged.** When framing your shot, take a good look at how the objects within the camera lens are arranged. Do they complement one another? Are there any points of interest the viewer can focus on? For example, tall objects, like trees, balance shorter objects, like a house or a bush. You can add interest to a picture of a flat, calm lake by zeroing in on a raft, boat, or the reeds growing along the shoreline. In many cases, you can spice up a potentially blah scene by tightening your focus on an element of the scene or shifting the camera angle.

Removing Parts of a Photograph

Finally, someone's snapped a really flattering picture of you. Unfortunately, you're sitting next to your long-since-ditched summer fling. Before you tear apart a perfectly good photograph, consider removing the image of the offending Romeo. (And if you are really bold, insert an image of someone much more interesting!)

Cropping works well when you want to remove an object or person that is near the edge of a photograph. But if your ex-beau is smack in the middle of the picture, cropping isn't the answer. For example, let's say the picture was taken at a family barbeque. Your ex-boyfriend was sitting between you and your brother, so if you crop the picture, you will cut out your brother too. What to do?

Open the picture in your editing program. Each is different but the instructions are generally the same.

1. Use the lasso masking tool to draw a mask around the person you want to remove from the picture. Do this very carefully so the mask only includes the area you want to eliminate. You may need to use the zoom tool to get into the tight spots.

2. Press CTRL+ X or the Delete key to remove the masked area.

Now, the boyfriend is gone. But you have a gaping hole that has to be filled with something. Try these options:

- Put something else there. For example, replace your ex with another person (see figure 13.1), an empty chair, or even the family dog. Take the replacement object from another part of the photograph, or from a different picture. But make sure it is in scale with the rest of the picture. Use the masking tool to draw an area around the replacement object, then copy and paste it to your photograph. We'll cover compositing, or putting different picture parts together, in more detail shortly.

- Fill in the hole with a solid color. If you're lucky, the picture has a solid background—a sparkling blue lake, not an American flag. If it does have a solid background, take the eyedropper tool and click it on the lake. Then use the fill (paint bucket) tool and click it on the empty space. The "lake" will appear to fill the empty hole.

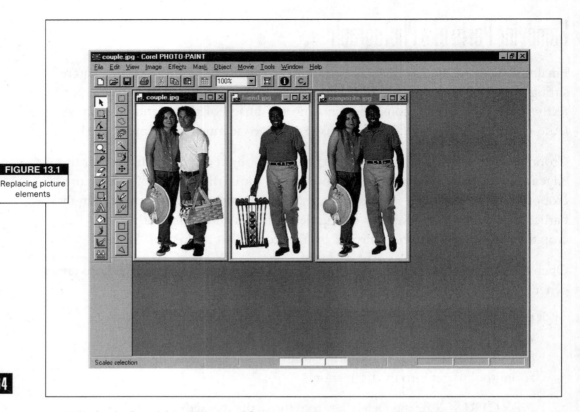

FIGURE 13.1
Replacing picture elements

- Fill the hole with a pattern. If you've got to try to reproduce the stripes on the flag, simply use the rectangle masking tool to enclose part of the flag. Then copy and paste the flag to a new file, crop the area outside of the pattern, and save the picture. When you return to the picture you're editing, you can usually select the flag's patterned image for the fill (paint bucket) tool instead of a color. It may not match perfectly, but you can come pretty close.

- Blend it in. You may be able to fill in the empty area by masking the background and using the lasso tool to blend the edges into your empty hole. We'll talk about blurs and other special effects later in this chapter.

Advanced touchups require a significant amount of patience—usually you have to get in and change the color of the individual pixels (dots) to refine your editing. But if you've got a picture you really want to salvage, or you want to try your hand at creating an entirely new scenario, it's worth the effort. There are also several software packages, like MetaCreations' Photo Soap (http://www.metacreations.com) that are relatively inexpensive (about $50) and offer really useful retouching tools.

Compositing Pictures

Compositing is a fancy term for putting parts of different pictures together, or replacing objects or people in one picture with objects or people from another picture. For example, Tony and Karen have a great photo of themselves and the kids relaxing in the living room. They'd like to send it to everyone in the family. Unfortunately, the absolutely hideous lamp Aunt Tonya sent them isn't in the picture and her feelings will be hurt if she doesn't see it. It's up to you to decide if you want to trick your own Aunt Tonya into thinking you admire her taste, but it's a snap to do it with digital compositing.

1. Open the picture you want to edit and use the Save As command to save it with a different name. This way, you still have the original picture.

2. Use the masking tool to select the lamp you really did put on your end table, delete it, then fill in or blend the empty area to match the background, as explained in the previous section.

3. Open a picture of Aunt Tonya's lamp. Use the masking tool to outline the ugly lamp—be sure to get around all those protrusions—then copy it to the clipboard.

4. Return to the main picture, paste the replacement lamp into the picture, and use the selection tool to position it.

5. Use the paintbrush tool to painstakingly touch up and blend the lamp into the picture. Aunt Tonya will be none the wiser.

Once you get going, have a little fun. Design photo collages, replace people's heads with horse or duck heads, and give life to just about anything you can think of.

165

Repairing Damaged Photographs

Although you cherish the pictures of your middle school buddies and the photo album of childhood memories your parents put together, time tends to introduce tears, fading, and other signs of damage. Fortunately, you can repair each picture by adjusting individual pixels so the whole image looks like new.

- Adjust the brightness, contrast, and color to give the picture an instant face-lift.

- Select sharpening options to make fuzzy and faded elements more distinct, and to bring out lines and edges. Experiment to get the effect you want.

- Use the paintbrush tool to blend in the edges of a torn photograph, eliminate water damage and fingerprint stains, or bring out faded features. You can adjust the paintbrush size and texture to suit your needs.

- Crop damaged areas out of a photograph if they aren't worth saving.

- Convert old color pictures to grayscale so they look like vintage black-and-white photographs.

Special Effects

So far, we've concentrated on fixing photographs that are somehow imperfect. But you can also use your artistic flair to convert average photographs into works of art. Most photo manipulation programs offer basic special-effects tools. You can also buy more sophisticated software that will enhance your special-effects repertoire in a big way: Play with color, create exciting patterns and textures, "morph" two or more images together, and more.

Making Duotone Photographs

Duotone photographs are similar to black-and-white photographs, but they use shades of color other than black. For example, you can use dark blue or purple for a subtle effect. Or use a warm, rich dark brown for an old-fashioned effect—the earliest photographs were printed in sepia tones (shades of brown) rather than black-and-white.

To transform your photograph into a duotone:

1. Open a picture and save it with a different name.

2. Convert your picture to a 256-color, grayscale image to make it look like a black-and-white photograph.

3. Convert the picture to an RGB color image. RGB stands for Red, Blue, and Green, the format used by color monitors. Notice this doesn't put the colors back in, but it does let you add them. You can't do that in grayscale mode.

4. Display your color-balance options (as explained in the section on color correction in chapter 12) and choose *one* color to replace the black. You can preview the image before applying the duotone.

Applying Filters

Special-effects tools are also called "filters" or "plug-ins." Imagine being able to make an ordinary photograph look like a Renoir or van Gogh painting. Or changing an image to make it look like you are seeing it through a keyhole or like it's on a page that is curling. You can also use filters to create custom backgrounds for your Web pages. Figure 13.2 shows just a few of the special effects you can apply to a picture.

WHAT ARE PLUG-INS?

Don't confuse special-effect plug-ins with Web-browser plug-ins (as explained in chapter 14). "Plug-in" is a generic term for any software created to extend another application's capabilities. Plug-ins don't generally run by themselves as an independent program. They are simply add-ons to an existing application. Kai's PowerTools, Black Box's Alien Skin, and other special-effect add-ons are image-program plug-ins. Shockwave, Real-Player, and other programs discussed in chapter 14 are Web-browser plug-ins.

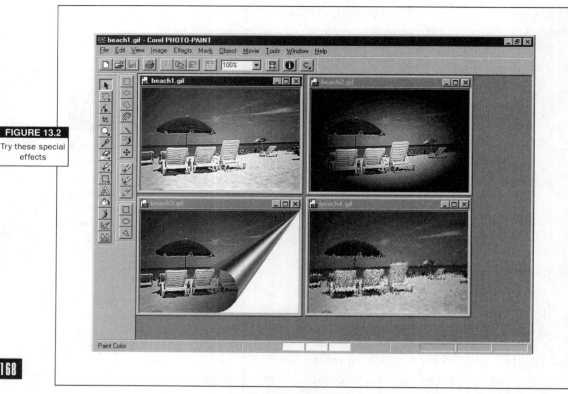

FIGURE 13.2

Try these special effects

168

Most image editing programs come with a few special-effects filters. For instance, you can apply a blur filter to create a soft-focus effect. Or you can make elements in the image stand out more with the sharpen filters. But you have to purchase the really good special-effects filters separately. One of the most popular special-effects programs is Kai's PowerTools by MetaCreations. It costs about $130 and many graphics and Web professionals swear by it. Xaos Tools also offers Paint Alchemy for about $125. You can find it in the AOL Computing Superstore (keyword: **CSS**), a graphics multimedia software area.

Special-effects software doesn't run as a stand-alone application. Instead, it's referred to as a plug-in, because it adds capabilities to image programs like PaintShop Pro, Corel PhotoPaint, and Adobe PhotoShop. When you install the software, the special effects are placed in a special plug-in folder in the image program directory. You'll also see them appear on the menu lists so you can select them easily.

To apply a special effect, use a masking tool to define the area for editing (it can be the entire picture). Let's say you want to convert a photograph to look like an

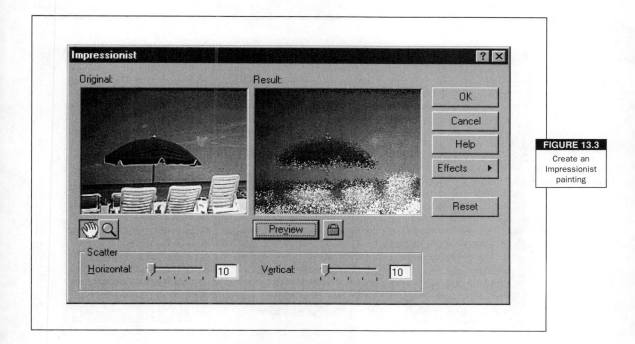

FIGURE 13.3

Create an
Impressionist
painting

Impressionist painting. Select the effect you want from the Effects or Filters menu (depending on your image program) to see a dialogue box similar to the one in figure 13.3. Special-effects dialogue boxes provide controls to help you determine how a special effect is applied, and then preview it.

Making Backgrounds and Textures

Many image programs come with ready-made textures and patterns you can customize and pour into masked areas of an image, using the fill tool. Some, like Kai's PowerTools, also help you build your own. First, open a new file with an image area 1 inch wide and 1 inch tall. Create a pattern or texture you like and click the fill tool on the image. Save and name it (patterns work best as BMPs or JPEGs). Now you can use the pattern as a background for pictures, presentations, or (if you've saved it as a JPEG) a Web page.

Morphing Pictures

Want to make silly faces, caricatures, or wildly distorted objects like the face shown in figure 13.4? "I'd have to be a really good artist," you might think. But all you really need is a program like MetaCreations PowerGoo, which costs about $50. You

169

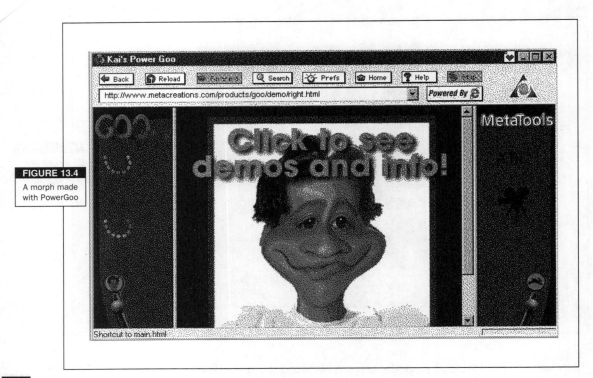

FIGURE 13.4

A morph made with PowerGoo

170

can create shapes, then overlay your photographs to distort them. Or you can blend two photographs together into one crazy picture. You can order Kai's PowerGoo from the AOL Store (keyword: **AOL Store**).

Create Buttons and 3D Text

Some special effects can also help you create beveled buttons, 3D text, and text with drop shadows, as shown in figure 13.5. Professional Web designers use these effects to add dimension to text and buttons for navigating a Web page. To create 3D or drop-shadowed text, open your image program, enter your text, select it with the magic wand masking tool, then select the Bevel or Drop Shadow filters. Some image programs let you mask all of the letters at once by holding down the Shift key and clicking the wand on each of them. With other programs, you'll have to apply the effect to each letter individually.

To create beveled buttons, use the circle or rectangle masking tool to define a shape and fill it with the color of your choice. Use the Bevel effect to make the edges look three-dimensional. Copy the button as many times as you need, and use the text tool to label them individually.

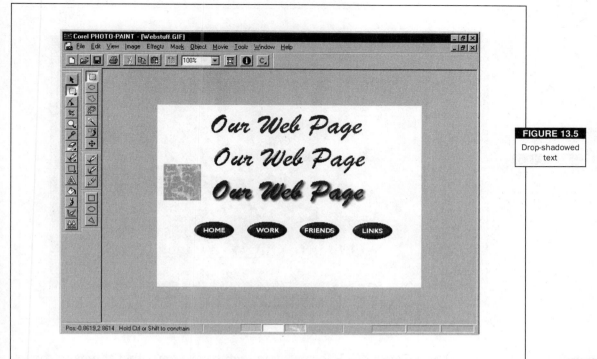

FIGURE 13.5

Drop-shadowed
text

Preparing Pictures for Web Pages

You can also use your image program and special-effects tools to create Web graphics or prepare your photographs for the Web. For example, the Web page shown in figure 13.6 uses some of the pictures and graphics you've seen in this chapter. Sure, you can download ready-made images from the PC Graphic Arts Forum (keyword: **PGR**), then insert and use them without changing them. But it's also possible to convert them to a Web-friendly GIF or JPEG format and edit them into your own piece of artwork (be sure you aren't using copyrighted material).

A Reminder about Resolution, Image Format, and File Size

When preparing photos and drawings for the Web, it is important to reduce the horizontal and vertical resolution to 96 dpi. That's all the Web can display; and 300 dpi images take forever to download. Don't forget to convert them to either GIF or JPEG format. Text, clip art, illustrations, and buttons look best as GIF files. Color and grayscale photographs, paintings, and detailed drawings look best as JPEGs.

FIGURE 13.6

Special effects on
a Web page

If you convert an image to GIF format, you then have a few other things to think about. First, do you want to use transparent GIFs (GIF 89s) or regular GIFs (GIF 87s)? Transparent GIFs are ideal for Web pages with patterned backgrounds—or those with background color different from the images. Why? Because you don't want the rectangular area around the image to display. You can usually create a transparent GIF by eliminating the image's background color. Most digital imaging programs have features for saving files as transparent GIFs.

When you save images as GIFs, you also need to think about whether to dither your colors. What's dithering? Dithering creates little dots to blend dissimilar areas of color together. Before JPEGs came along, people dithered their GIF files to create photo-realistic images. Now that you can use JPEGs, there's no reason to dither GIFs, which can't display colors boldly. JPEGS can compress to smaller file sizes too!

In fact, you usually *won't* want your GIF images to dither, so you need to select browser-safe colors. GIFs are indexed color files, limited to the 256 colors on your system's color palette. Only 216 of the 256 colors on your system palette display correctly in a Web browser. The others are displayed as annoying little dots instead of solid areas of color. PaintShop Pro comes with a browser-safe color palette that converts your image's color to the right colors.

Finally, you should pay attention to your file sizes. The images you use on a single Web page shouldn't add up to more than 50 KB or so. Otherwise, your Web page may take too long to download. But don't compress any individual image *too* much, or it won't look very presentable. Most image programs provide options for compressing JPEGs. "Medium" quality generally gets good results.

We'll talk more about preparing your images for use online in chapter 15.

14

GRAPHICS AND MULTIMEDIA ONLINE

If you aren't yet intrigued by multimedia, it won't be long before you are. After all, you already enjoy multimedia effects when you hear that familiar phrase "you've got mail" or watch an animated character blink its way across a Web page. Maybe you've even watched an online video presentation or two. But now we're talking about using your digital pictures to create your *own* feature presentations.

You don't need fancy hardware or costly software, and it doesn't require a lot of memory or a fast processing speed. Furthermore, most of the sound and animation files you will ever want to create are small

176

compared to some of the video presentations you'll find online. This is important to note because most of us use regular 28.8 Kbps modems, and downloading enormous files can feel like sipping the Pacific Ocean through a straw. Rest assured, new technologies are putting video and other resource-hungry multimedia within everyone's reach. Check out the new 56 Kbps modems. Many now cost under $150 at the Modem Shop on AOL (keyword: **Modem Shop**).

You can add multimedia to your Web page, send files as e-mail attachments, and download and upload all kinds of files in various forum and channel areas. And the Web browser on the AOL service is Internet Explorer, so you can take advantage of cutting-edge technologies like Shockwave, RealPlayer, and VDOLive to start enjoying multimedia right away.

Downloading and Distributing Digital Pictures and Multimedia Online

Here are just a few of the things you can download and distribute online:

- **Digital pictures.** Of course, you'll want to exchange digital pictures and display them on your Web page. Start off with a trip to the PC Graphic Arts Forum at keyword **PGR.**

- **Business materials.** With today's tools— like Microsoft's Word, Excel, and PowerPoint assistants and Adobe Acrobat—

you can distribute business documents on the Web. These programs come with special viewers people can use to see your files even if they don't have the program you used to create them. You can get Adobe Acrobat by visiting the Adobe area at keyword **Adobe**. (Microsoft Assistants are available from http://www.microsoft.com).

- **Animations.** The forums on AOL and the Web are filled with GIF animations you can download. They're fun to look at and easy to create. You can also view cutting-edge games and works of art, including Shockwave movies, with plug-ins included with your Web browser. Drop by the Animations and Video Forum at keyword **A&V Forum**.

- **Sound files.** The AOL service abounds with sound files you can enjoy— everything from simple music clips and wacky noises to sophisticated online radio broadcasts. It is surprisingly inexpensive and easy to make your own sound files. Stop by the SoundRoom (keyword: **SoundRoom**) for lots of great sound clips.

- **Video.** You can use video files to create everything from home movies to high-end product demonstrations for your small business. The Real-Player plug-in even lets you view video broadcasts online with an ordinary modem and computer. If you'd like to create videos of your own and distribute them online, you'll need to spend a little money and time. But it isn't as hard or expensive as you might think. The Entertainment channel at keyword **Entertainment** offers interactive movie reviews with video clips.

Digital Pictures and Multimedia in E-mail Messages

Perhaps the most popular way to distribute your multimedia files online is by attaching them to your e-mail messages. It's easy if you use files that are smaller than 250 K. As you've learned, you can even embed a digital picture directly in the message. But if you are going to attach a digital picture file, make sure the person on the receiving end has an AOL account or the application she needs to open your file. She can open GIFs and JPEGs in a browser, or PCX and BMP files in her Windows Paint program. TIF files require an image program like PhotoShop or PhotoPaint.

Digital Pictures and Multimedia in AOL Forums

More and more members are uploading their digital pictures to designated areas on the AOL service. For example, there's the Portrait Gallery (keyword: **Gallery**), where you can download and view pictures of other AOL members and their families. Or you can upload your own. You can also exchange files on the Multimedia gallery (keyword: **A&V Forum**), the Computer channel (keyword: **Computers**), the Photography forum (keyword: **Photography Forum**), Kids Only (keyword: **Kids Only**), and many other areas.

But first, you need to know how to upload and download picture files. It's simple. To download files, visit the forum or channel areas where files are posted, and:

1. Select a picture file from the list (don't forget to keep clicking on More until the button fades).

2. Click on Read Description to find out more about the contents, and to make sure you have the right software to view it.

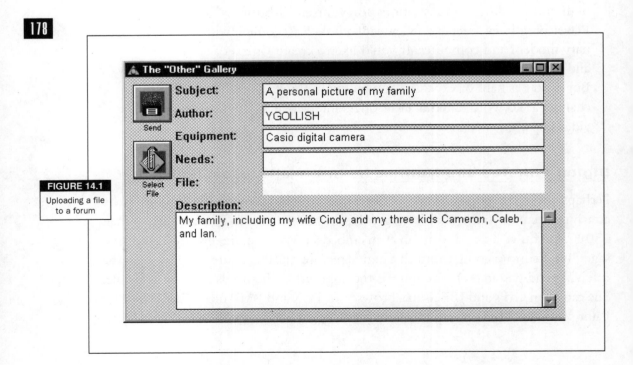

FIGURE 14.1
Uploading a file
to a forum

3. If the file type is supported by AOL's software (and most of them are), the file opens automatically when it finishes downloading. Otherwise, you can open it with a separate application (files download to the default directory, probably C:\AOL4\Download directory).

Many forums also allow you to post your own picture file. Make sure you check out the Read Me file to get a handle on the rules and the types of files you can post. Then, just click on Upload to post your file.

A dialogue box like the one shown in figure 14.1 will request your screen name, the name of the file, the application or hardware you used to create it, and whether someone needs special software to view it. When you finish entering your information, click on the Select File button to add your file, then click on the Send button to upload it to the area.

We should also mention that sometimes the posting areas are full. When this happens, the Upload button looks indistinct and you can't select it. Don't worry, the forum administrator will soon create a new posting area on the forum.

On the World Wide Web

179

You can download, view, and play an assortment of interesting multimedia files from pages on the World Wide Web. Some multimedia files launch straight from a Web page, while other files download when you click on a link. Remember, never download a file from the Web unless you are confident it does not contain a virus, and always make sure you have permission to use someone else's pictures on your Web page or documents.

One of the easiest ways to get a picture from a Web page is simply to click the right mouse button on it and select the Save Picture As option from the pop-up menu. This trick can come in handy when you want to add a picture of a friend or online pal to a Web page you're creating and she happens to have a picture of herself on her own Web page.

If you want to upload picture files to your own personal Web page, use Personal Publisher as discussed in chapter 7. This simple Web page tool is great for getting you started. It also automatically uploads your pages for you. But, if you'd like to create Web pages that give you more control over your layouts and that support advanced features like frames and multimedia. Just download AOLpress, which we'll talk about later in this chapter.

Using GIF Animations

When surfing the Web, you'll frequently find that people have used an animated GIF to get your attention. Quite simply, animations are created by rapidly displaying a sequence of small GIF pictures, just as classic animation is created by displaying a sequence of still drawings. Animations are the simplest and easiest way for you to create your own multimedia files from digital pictures.

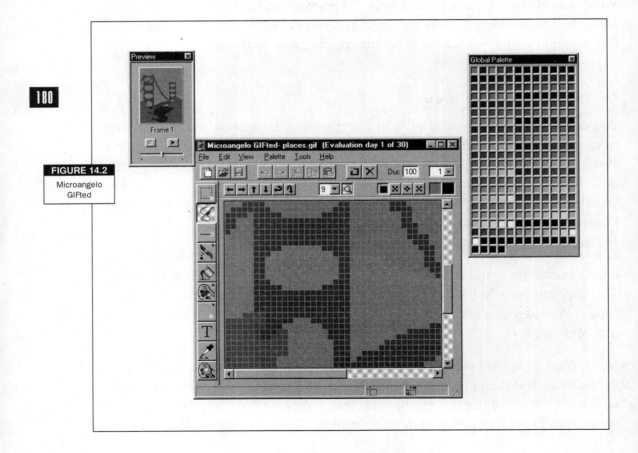

FIGURE 14.2

Microangelo
GIFted

180

If you're a budding artist and want to try your hand at GIF animations, try a program like Microangelo GIFted (see figure 14.2), available on the Computer channel (keyword: **Computers**). It's inexpensive, easy to use, and even comes with a special QuickStart manual. The program also provides a large set of drawing and editing tools to create and change your artwork.

GIFted's main window is the drawing screen. Another window provides a selection of colors that can be blended and changed. And a Preview window shows the results of your work as they'll appear in the animation. You can play the animation in the Preview window as you complete the frames. Each animation frame is a separate GIF picture file.

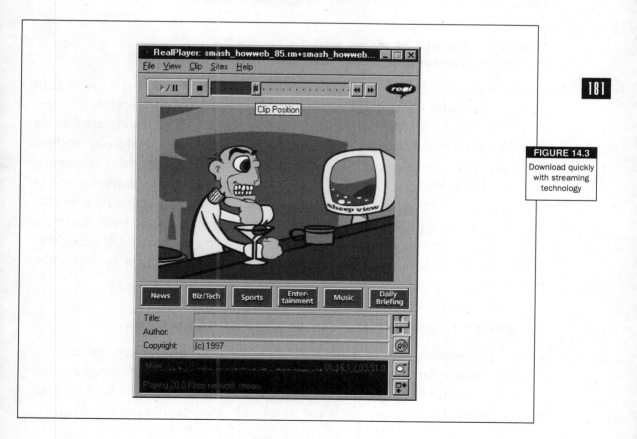

FIGURE 14.3

Download quickly with streaming technology

Using Professional-Quality Multimedia Files

When the Web first became popular, starving artists and corporate CEOs alike got excited about the possibility of distributing multimedia via the Web. Alas, they ran into one major problem. High-end audio, video, and animation take forever to download. Even the smallest multimedia files are much larger than text and image files. Fortunately, RealNetworks has come up with a good solution: *streaming multimedia*. With streaming multimedia, the files play *while* they're downloading instead of only after they finish downloading. This makes it possible to distribute very large multimedia files over the AOL service and the Internet. In fact, RealNetworks has broadcast live audio and video concerts, games, and other events.

What do you need to enjoy streaming multimedia? The free RealPlayer, shown in figure 14.3. You can download the latest version of this, and other plug-ins, from the Multimedia Showcase (keyword: **Multimedia Showcase**).

Macromedia Shockwave and Flash Animations, Presentations, and Graphics

Shockwave is one of the most popular multimedia technologies on the Internet. In fact, it's so popular, it's included automatically with the Microsoft Internet Explorer Web browser, which is also part of the AOL 4.0 software. When Shockwave files are created, they're called "movies" because the software programs used to create them (such as Macromedia Director and Authorware) model the results after that popular format. Multimedia developers use the movies to create complex, informative—or simply entertaining—presentations, animations, and games. In addition, Shockwave can display digital pictures, illustrations, and layouts created with Macromedia's Freehand drawing program. Whenever you browse the Internet, there's a very good chance you'll run into Shockwave-produced animations on business Web pages.

Creating Shockwave Movies and Flash Animations

Creating Shockwave movies requires an investment of time, money, and training because Director and Authorware are costly and complex multimedia programs. But software programs like Macromedia Flash, on the other hand, make animating your digital pictures far more affordable and simple. Flash animations can also display in the RealPlayer, if you want to stream them. For samples of Flash animations, visit the Multimedia Showcase (keyword: **Multimedia Showcase**)

Creating Your Own Multimedia Presentations

Multimedia professionals can surely knock your socks off with their high-budget productions. But let's say you and your band want to expand your exposure on the Web. You can post some of your songs and a video clip even if your budget hasn't hit the big time.

Creating your own RealMedia broadcasts or high-quality video or sound productions would require expensive audio and video equipment, technical expertise, and access to a RealNetworks server. And who's going to bother waiting for a 5 MB video to download? Fortunately, you can still use programs like HotDog Pro to add streaming multimedia to your Web site. It's an excellent Web page editor that costs about $100 and comes with a special RealMedia tool to convert AVI movies and WAV sound files to the RealPlayer format. While you won't get the professional quality you'll find on RealNetworks' Web site, it might be just what you need to get your gig in gear.

183

Online Audio

Of all the various multimedia elements we've just mentioned, sound is without a doubt the most popular. You'll have noticed by now that the AOL service uses sound as prompts, greetings, and notifications when you're online. Your Web browser supports most of the common sound file formats on the Web, including WAV, MIDI, and AU files. Sound is one of those things that everyone can play around with on their computer, even if they've never played a note of music in their lives. All you need is a sound card (most computers come with them these days). A microphone helps too.

The terms used in online audio can be confusing. There are four key things to keep in mind when you think about sound:

- The process of recording sound is usually referred to as *sampling*. Now, if someone ever runs this term by you again, you can act unimpressed and say, "So what? I know what *that* means!"

- When computers record and play sound, the measurement of quality is often called the *sampling rate*.

- How is the sampling rate determined? By using a simple measurement: *kilohertz,* indicating the rate of thousands of samples per second. For example, 11 kilohertz (kHz) refers to the fact that a sound was recorded or sampled at the rate of 11,000 times a second. If that sounds really fast, it is. However, it's not fast enough to create good sound files.

- Sound quality is also determined by something called *bit depth*. That is how many computer bits make up each of those samples per second! There are two settings: 8-bit and 16-bit. Sixteen-bit creates much better sound quality than 8-bit, but takes up twice as much space.

Eight-bit, 22 kHz sound files are typically used for games and online applications. Sixteen-bit, 44 kHz sound files offer CD-quality sound. If you want to record verbal greetings and notes for important data files you send to people (which you can very easily do), you'll very likely use the 8-bit, 22 kHz setting because it's economical yet produces listenable quality. Anything else is either too big or or too poor in quality to be practical when downloading or distributing sound files online.

When you bought your computer, it almost certainly came with a sound card or a sound chip built onto the motherboard. If that's the case, you'll also have received a microphone with your computer. That's really all you need to record your own audio files. If you would like a more in-depth discussion on how to do fun things with audio software, read Rich Grace's *The Sound and Music Workshop*. The AOL store has a good selection of the most popular sound cards from Voyetra, Creative Labs, and others (keyword **Hardware Center**; then select multimedia).

About MIDI

MIDI (musical instrument digital interface) sound files are the most suitable for representing music (as opposed to SoundBlaster-compatible files, which reproduce the blasts and explosions so popular in online games). The browser on the AOL service allows you to listen to any MIDI files you encounter on the AOL service on the

Internet. But if you're a musician, you might want to create your own. To get started, take a peek at the back of your computer, where you'll probably see a 15-pin connector (it's the one you use to connect your joystick). That connector also serves as a MIDI port.

With the right adapter you can hook up any MIDI instrument, such as a synthesizer keyboard or a guitar, to that sound card port on your computer. Then you can use the instrument to control and play sounds from the synthesizer chip on your sound card. It's that chip that determines how those songs are going to sound on your PC.

MIDI files are great for online applications because a typical three- or four-minute song only takes up about 50 K or 60 K of space. In contrast, a stereo CD quality sound file will eat up approximately 10 M of space. MIDI files also play automatically online, at CD-quality levels, if you've got the right plug-in software (discussed later in this chapter).

Recording Sounds

The quickest way to experiment with multimedia sound is to use the built-in Sound Recorder on Windows 95. To start it up, click the Start button, select Programs, then Accessories, Multimedia, and finally Sound Recorder (see figure 14.4). You'll have to load and play WAV files, because Sound Recorder won't play MIDI files.

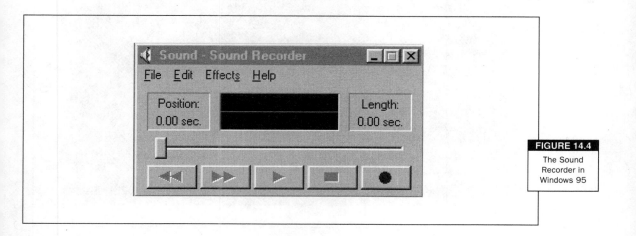

FIGURE 14.4

The Sound Recorder in Windows 95

Assuming you have a microphone hooked up to your sound card and that everything else is set up properly:

1. Click on the record button (the one with the red dot).

2. When you're finished recording, click on the stop button (the one with the square).

3. Click on the seek to start button at the bottom left of the Sound Recorder to "rewind" the sound (the one with the two left-pointing arrows).

4. Click on the play button to listen to your creation (the one with the single right-pointing arrow).

5. To save your work, pull down the File menu and select Save.

186

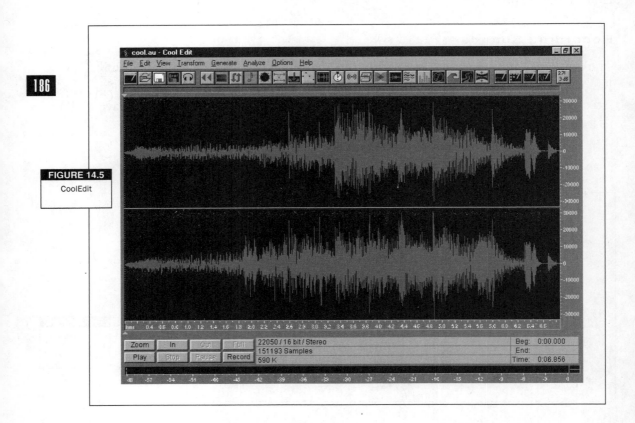

FIGURE 14.5
CoolEdit

With Sound Recorder, you can:

- Insert a second sound file at any point in the currently loaded file.

- Copy the entire sound onto the Windows clipboard and then edit it or paste it into another program.

- Increase or decrease the volume of the sound.

- Increase or decrease the speed, or tempo, of the sound.

- Change the quality of the recorded sound if you need to save space (this is often called *downsampling*).

You have other options for editing and changing sounds besides the features offered in Windows. One of the best programs you can play around with is called CoolEdit (see figure 14.5). You can find it in the shareware library on the AOL service for about $50 (keyword: **software**), then search Shareware for CoolEdit.

CoolEdit will let you copy or cut and paste any part or all of a sound file into another—a great way to create something unique. You can also add dozens of different effects, including echo, reverb, distortion, amplifying, compression, and delay. You can even reduce the noise levels originally recorded into a sound file.

VDOLive, AVI, and QuickTime Videos

When surfing the Web, you'll frequently come across VDOLive, AVI, and Quick-Time videos. VDOLive is a plug-in offered by VDONet, a company specializing in streaming video broadcasting. As with RealPlayer, the VDOLive plug-in lets you view exciting, high-quality video clips and broadcasts without time-consuming downloads. And because both of these cutting-edge technologies come with your AOL browser, you'll never have to miss out on any broadcast. AVI movies are also popular on the Web. If you have a video camera and software like QuickCam, you can also create your own AVI movies and add them to your Web page.

Finally, there's QuickTime. QuickTime is an Apple multimedia technology that has been around for quite a while. Apple's superb multimedia extensions for Windows and Macintosh environments are used to play video and MIDI files, and help you turn your digital pictures into multimedia works of art. You can download the QuickTime plug-in from the Multimedia Showcase (keyword: **Multimedia Show-case**).

187

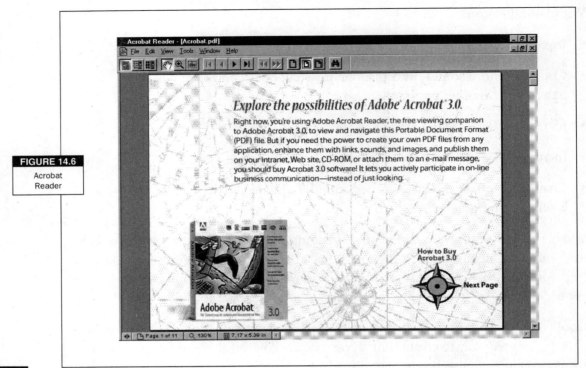

FIGURE 14.6

Acrobat
Reader

188

Using Your Digital Pictures in Documents Online

Does your business have a lot of brochures or other materials you'd like to distribute online? It can get a bit tricky because you want people to view your digital pictures and special fonts exactly the way you laid them out, even if they don't have the same fonts and programs you do.

Fortunately, many popular programs come with utilities that let other people view your files online—even if they don't have the same program. The ones you'll come across most frequently are files that require Microsoft Office Viewer plug-ins or Adobe Acrobat Reader.

If you use your digital pictures in Microsoft Office applications like Word, Excel, and PowerPoint, you now have an easy way to let non–Microsoft Office users look at them. Microsoft offers free viewers from their Web site at http://www.microsoft. com so now you can send people the file with the viewer. You can also put your files on your Web page and provide a link to the viewer application. Of course, this still doesn't solve the problem of fonts. But you can avoid problems by sticking with fonts that almost everyone has, like Arial and Times New Roman.

Adobe Acrobat is a lifesaver for people in the graphic arts community who put a lot of time and effort into creating their designs, choosing their fonts, and illustrating or photographing their digital pictures for the Web. The program, which costs about $500, enables users to convert documents and illustrations to a Portable Document Format (PDF) file. People who have neither the application the document was gen-

FIGURE 14.7
AOLpress

erated on with the fonts, nor Acrobat, can download Acrobat Reader for free from Adobe's Web site (keyword: **Adobe**) and use it to view PDF files. In fact, if you visit the IRS online, you'll notice they've used Acrobat to format their downloadable tax forms!

When you click a link to download a PDF file, Acrobat Reader launches, as shown in figure 14.6. Its simple toolbar buttons and controls let you move backward and forward in the document and from page to page. It's a good idea to have this tool on your hard drive because Acrobat-formatted documents are widely available online and many companies offer downloadable documentation for their computer products in this format.

Bringing It All Together with AOLPress

Clearly, if you want to enhance your digital pictures with multimedia effects online, there's a broad range of possibilities. When you are ready to start creating sophisticated Web pages, turn to AOLPress, the freeware Web-page design tool on the AOL service (see figure 14.7). You can incorporate sound files, GIF animations, Flash animations, and QuickTime video.

AOLPress is a WYSIWYG (What You See Is What You Get) Web page editor that makes combining special effects with your digital pictures as easy as using a standard word processing, graphics, or presentation program. You can also add features like GIF animations, Acrobat documents, Shockwave movies, and RealPlayer objects such as Flash animations to your Web pages. If ever there was a place to be creative, this is it!

15

STORING AND KEEPING TRACK OF PICTURES

The more you enjoy using digital pictures and multimedia, the more you'll realize that they take up a lot of space and can be hard to keep track of. Whether you use digital pictures at work or for fun, it's important to create a system for storing and archiving them. The more images and multimedia you create, the more backup capability you need. Start with something as simple as a few floppy disks or the inexpensive and popular Zip drive, or purchase a high-end, 2 gigabyte (GB) removable drive or a writable CD-ROM at the AOL Store. The important thing is that you organize your digital pictures, print them out, and store them so you can get at them easily. This chapter covers a variety of storage options to suit just about every need, and tricks for keeping track of your pictures.

Storage Options

As we've already discussed briefly in chapter 10, you have an incredibly broad array of choices for storing your data. First, your computer already comes with two different types of storage: a floppy disk drive and a hard drive (the main storage unit of your system). If you've bought a brand-new computer, it is possible it will have a Zip drive built in. But this is just the beginning.

Removable drives come in all shapes and sizes, from the 100 MB Zip drives just mentioned to writable CD drives, 1 GB and 2 GB Jaz drives, SyJet and EzFlyer from SyQuest, and many others. Tape drives are another popular and practical option for archiving huge numbers of files and creating complete backups of your system.

We'll start this chapter by describing the most important storage device in your computer—your system's hard disk. You probably don't even think about it. It's just an invisible component to you, but it's of crucial importance.

Hard Disks

A lot of things have happened in the disk drive market over the last few years. They're cheaper, faster, and larger than ever. If you're so inclined and can do a little shopping around, you can buy an 8 GB hard disk for your PC for less than $500. Start with the Hardware Shop at the AOL Store (keyword: **AOL Store**).

Why are these huge hard disks so cheap? The technology has advanced a lot, competition is intense, and companies are desperate to keep moving ahead and selling product. Users benefit because their systems are cheaper and more usable than ever. They're also becoming more reliable, on the average.

If you're in the market for a new computer, the minimum size hard disk on your system should be 2.5 GB. Most mail-order manufacturers won't sell systems with less than 3 GB, because smaller hard disks are just too cheap now, and companies can't make money on them. The sweet spot is now 2.5 to 4 GB. It's hard to find enough current, compelling PC applications to fill up a hard disk of that size, unless you copy entire games from CD-ROM disks. If you decide to start doing a lot of imaging and multimedia stuff with your computer, you'll find ways to use up that space over time. Fortunately, it's cheap and relatively easy to buy more disk space for your machine when you need it. One possible solution, especially for imaging, is to consider buying a removable drive, our next topic.

Zip, Jaz, and SyQuest Drives

Jason, Ann, and their kids decided to give the relatives a special homemade gift—a calendar with pictures of everyone in the family. To make everything extra special, they decided to take the calendar to a professional printer. But yikes! The calendar file is too large to fit on a disk. Fortunately, they have a Zip drive and so does the printer. Jason copied the calendar onto a Zip disk, brought it to the printer, and the gifts were ready a week later.

The easiest way to store your files is to use a removable drive. Removable drives attach to your computer and work similarly to floppy disks. You can just stick the

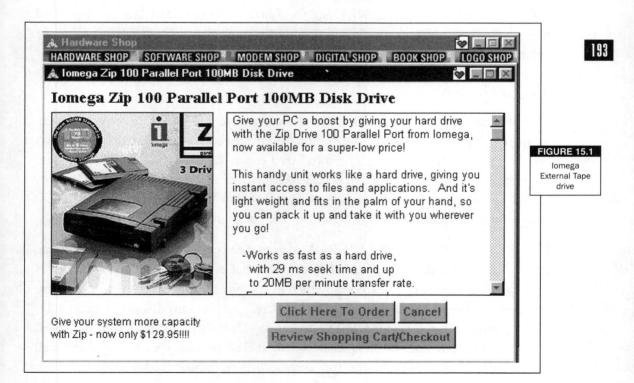

FIGURE 15.1
Iomega
External Tape
drive

cartridge in and move files back and forth between computers. You can even view and work with pictures directly from the cartridge, without transferring them to your computer. Most of the products mentioned here are available at the Hardware Shop in the AOL Store (keyword: **AOL Store**).

The most popular removable drive is Iomega's Zip drive (figure 15.1). Zip drives cost less than $200, and each cartridge (about $15) holds 100 MB worth of digital pictures. Zip drives also come in handy when you need to exchange large files with other people. Many new computers even come with them built in.

Iomega also makes a 1 GB Jaz drive and a 2 GB Jaz II. These drives cost a couple hundred dollars more, but come in handy for people who have lots of large files. And digital pictures tend to be large. Since Jaz drives hold more information than many people's hard drive, they can also double as a backup system for your computer.

Syquest also makes reliable backup drives. Though not as popular, they give you more bang for the buck. The EZ Flier costs only a little more than the Zip drive and holds 250 MB of data. The SyJet lists for a little less than the 1 GB Jaz drive and holds 1.5 GB of information. If you don't need to exchange files with other people often, the Syquest drives could be a good bet.

About CD-ROM Drives

Now almost everyone has a CD-ROM drive. Average CD-ROM drives vary in performance, but cost a hundred dollars for the current models. They don't add much cost to a system, and in fact it's hard to buy a computer now that doesn't have one. One thing you'll notice about new CD-ROM drives is the word *variable*. It means that if you see someone advertising a CD-ROM that has 24X speed or 32X speed, that is the *peak* speed of the CD drive, not the constant speed.

Here's what that means. Old CD-ROM drives, the very first ones ever made, were called "single-speed." The practical effect was that single-speed CD-ROM drives could read disks at 150 K a second, which in the present day is very slow and is the baseline against which all other CD-ROM drives are measured. Lots of older CD-ROM drives run at 2X speed (300 K/second), 4X (600 K/second), and 8X speed (1200 K/second). The fastest ones now run at 24X or 32X speeds, but they're all called *variable-speed* CD-ROMs for a reason. A variable-speed CD-ROM drive doesn't always run at 24X or 32X speed yet. The lowest speed of a variable-speed CD-ROM drive is usually something like 8X or 12X speed. Older CD-ROM drives, rated at 4X or 6X and so on, run at their speeds consistently.

Using Writable CD-ROMs

Jody is an administrator in a busy sales office that produces lots of presentations and brochures. Everyone depends on her when they look for, say, that photograph that Andy used in his report about seven months ago. All the offices and cubicles are computer networked, and Jody has a very special task: She has to back up special directories on everyone's computer onto a writable CD-ROM drive attached to her computer. She does this three times a week, and she's become very good at it. Each person's computer has a separate CD-ROM labeled with the user's name, and Jody uses them to back up their critical data files.

To help people keep track of digital pictures, drawings, presentations, spreadsheets, and other files, Jody has set up procedures requiring everyone to save certain files to assigned directories.

Suddenly, someone's hard disk crashes. The network manager comes in and replaces the hard disk and sets it up with the user's programs so the user can get back to work. Fortunately, Jody had just made a complete backup of all the user's vital data the evening before. The user has only lost a couple of hours' work. All Jody needs to do is slap the CD-RW disk containing the user's latest information into the user's computer's CD-ROM drive, and data restoration is done in a matter of minutes! This is a lot easier than restoring computer data from a tape drive.

Writable CD-ROMs have other advantages too. People in the office can save and catalog images they plan to use again. Many of them even use a thumbnail program (as explained later in the "Archiving Your Picture Collection" section of this chapter) to print out miniature versions of each picture and its filename. They then slip the printout into the CD-ROM case for easy reference.

Normal CDs, of course, aren't writable. You can only view these files on your computer, so what are you supposed to do? Buy a rewritable CD-ROM drive. There are two terms to know: CD-R and CD-RW.

CD-ROMs have great advantages as a backup medium. They hold enough to be useful (up to 650 megabytes). They're universal (even more than Zip drives), because every PC out there that's been made in the last three or four years has a CD-ROM drive, and PCs usually require a CD-ROM drive in order to install software. If you ever make your own CD-ROMs, anyone out there can read them. That's incredibly powerful. They don't hold as much as a Jaz or SyJet disk, but many more people have CD-ROM drives.

CD-R stands for CD-Recordable. CD-Rs are not read-only memory drives like CD-ROMs. The big difference is that CD-Rs allow you to write exactly once to any CD disk media that's compatible with the drive. CD-Rs are best used when you have to write a large amount of information to any one disk (several hundred megabytes at least). Otherwise, you wind up wasting a lot of space on a given CD-R disk. If a mistake happens during the write to a disk (the computer switches off for some reason, crashes, or bad data occurs), the entire disk is wasted. Though the disks are cheap, the CD-R solution isn't very efficient. It's also a bit harder for inexperienced users to handle. Presently, CD-Rs are starting to disappear as their more-advanced CD-RW counterpart becomes popular, for good reason.

CD-RWs are a big advance from CD-Rs. CD-RW (which stands for CD-ReWritable) drives allow multiple reads and writes to the same disk, and behave very much like other removable drives, though they're a lot slower. You can erase data from a CD-RW disk just as you would with other kinds of removable disks. There's no wasted space with CD-RW, and if a mistake occurs, you can just start over with the same disk. Of all the possible storage solutions, a CD-RW drive is among the most versatile and practical. You can find one for around $400. Check out the AOL Store (keyword: **Hardware Center**; then select Storage) for CD-RWs.

Typically, CD-RWs operate at varying speeds. Most write data at 2X speeds (300 K a second, twice the rate of an old single-speed CD-ROM drive), perform records at 2X speed, and can read data from a disk at 4X or 6X speeds. So, CD-RWs actually combine the functions of three different types of drives (ReWriteable, Recordable, and Read-Only Memory). More expensive drives can write at 4X speeds, but you pay a premium.

Because prices are dropping, this is rapidly becoming a great option for anyone. The drives are fairly costly, but the disks are dirt cheap, even compared to tape, which is discussed next.

Speaking of backing up…

Being Safe with Tape Backup

Nowadays, computers are coming out with 5 GB hard drives, and more. You can store an awful lot of digital pictures in there. But how can you back up a system like that? Doing backups once a week or so is very important for the long-term health of your computer. If something goes wrong with your computer, a backup lets you restore your system to the way it was. For people who have a 2 GB Jaz drive and a computer that holds 1 MB, backing up is easy. They can copy all of their files to a Jaz drive cartridge. Some people even use Zip disks for backups. But that could get almost as bad as using floppies. Just think. You'd need 450 Zip disks to back up a 6.4 GB hard drive. Imagine how long that would take!

Yet, you need some way to make backups. It'd be nice to keep costs down, too. If you want to do those things, there's only one good option: tape backup. Fortunately, tape drives are starting to catch up to modern hard drives, allowing you to back up your entire system onto only one or two high-capacity tapes. There are some confusing terms involved with tape backups, but everything important is explained here.

First of all, tape drives are the most cost-effective way to do complete backups of your system. It's remotely possible to use a SyJet or Jaz drive to do it, but backup software doesn't usually support those devices, and the disks cost a lot more than tapes. Tape backup drives have advanced a lot in the last year or so.

There is one major disadvantage to tape drives, which has to do with the way tapes work: They're relatively slow and you can't get to your files as easily as you can with a removable or hard disk. Tape backup devices write information in a very long sequence. Because of this, you can't just open up a tape on a tape drive and view the files or directories as icons. Instead, you've got to rewind or move forward as you would an audio tape cassette. Tape drives are meant truly as backups; you make a second copy of your entire system onto one or two tapes and store the tapes away in case of a disaster.

The best high-capacity tape drives use a tape cartridge called Travan. There are several flavors of Travan tapes. The smallest and oldest ones are called TR-1, and they can hold 400 megabytes of data. If you can compress your data as you back it up, the TR-1 tapes can hold a maximum of 800 megabytes. In practice, they don't hold that much.

When you back your system up onto tapes, usually you'll want to *compress* the information during backup to save tape space. Compressing the information doesn't mean you'll lose anything; it's just done so that your backup takes a bit less time and doesn't use as many tapes. When you buy a tape drive for your Windows 95 or Windows 98 system, normally it will come with some kind of useful backup software that allows you to select compression for your backups when desired. If you back up uncompressed data, the backup process will take a little less time but will also use more tapes.

The newest tape drives, like the ones discussed here, use a new Travan tape called TR-4. This is the type to get, especially if you have a brand-new computer with a large hard drive. Travan TR-4 tape cartridges can hold up to 4 GB *uncompressed*. Drives using this cartridge tend to be more expensive but are state-of-the-art for consumer backup devices. They include the HP SureStore T4i and the Exabyte Eagle's Nest TR-4i. If you've just bought a computer with one of those ultra-big hard drives, consider getting one of these.

The Iomega Ditto Tape Drive, shown in figure 15.2, lets you archive up to 3.2 GB on a single tape. In practice, it'll probably be a little less, but for most backup jobs this is more than sufficient. Best of all, at $150, you can't beat the price.

One important thing to keep in mind is the quality of the backup software that comes with the tape drive. Does it run under Windows 95? Is it fairly easy to use and understand? For example, Iomega does a pretty good job making its bundled software simple to use for either removable drives or tape drives. Many other manufacturers bundle some kind of backup software with their products. You can also go to computer stores and buy special backup software programs that allow for more features than the software that's included with your drive.

There's another key tool you should know about, and this time it's software: archiving software. Usually, archiving software is used to help you organize large collections of image files, do mass file conversions, rename collections of files, and do many other highly useful tasks. Whether you use tapes, removable drives, or nothing at all except what's already installed on your system, you need some kind of software that allows you to track and manage your work. We'll tell you how to archive your picture collection next.

Hardware Shop

HARDWARE SHOP | SOFTWARE SHOP | MODEM SHOP | DIGITAL SHOP | BOOK SHOP | LOGO SHOP

Iomega Ditto 2GB External Tape Drive

Iomega Ditto 2GB External Tape Drive

Want to give your PC a little insurance? Then back it up with the Ditto 2GB External Tape Drive from Iomega! This portable light-weight drive is the perfert backup solution for multiple locations.

Back up to 2GB of compressed or 1GB uncompressed data while you work with just the click of a button. Plus moving files from tape to disk or disk to tape takes just seconds! Ideal for home or office use!

-Supports standard and
 enhanced parallel ports.

Incredible price break - now just $149.99!

Click Here To Order   Cancel

Review Shopping Cart/Checkout

FIGURE 15.2

Tape backup device

Archiving Your Picture Collection

You can learn a lot from people who work with digital pictures for a living. A typical example is Ross, a graphic artist, who has to keep track of hundreds of images. He can't give his pictures easy-to-remember names like "charlie-at-beach.tif" because the people who use his files don't know who Charlie is. Instead, he has to name them something like "chap01004.tif." Yuck.

How does Ross keep track of all of those pictures? He uses a *thumbnail* program. It displays thumbnails—miniatures—of all images in a selected folder or on a disk. All Ross has to do is launch the program and open a folder to get a quick glimpse of his pictures. If he needs to check one of them, he can click on an image to display it at full size. The Picture Gallery (keyword: **Gallery**) is a simple thumbnail program.

More advanced thumbnail programs also let you print thumbnails with filenames and convert large numbers of images to different file formats at once.

What does Ross do when he finishes a project? He goes out for a nice dinner, breathes a sigh of relief, and takes all the images off of his hard drive to leave room for the next project. But he can't just dump them in the Recycle Bin. He might have to make revisions in a few weeks. Instead, he moves the files to his Zip drive, and prints out an image catalog with his thumbnail program. He then labels the Jaz cartridge, places it in a manila envelope with the printout, labels the envelope, and puts it in his file cabinet.

You probably don't have to deal with as many pictures as Ross. But it's still nice to keep the ones you have organized and easily accessible. Digital pictures have a way of multiplying. Before you know it, you've got hundreds of photographs on your computer and can't find the ones you want when you need them. What can you do? You need an image management program. With the right software, you can solve all these minor problems with ease. It doesn't have to be expensive, and you can get the programs you need right off the World Wide Web or from AOL's software libraries.

ThumbsPlus

There are many programs around to help you archive your images. But Cerious Software's ThumbsPlus, as shown in figure 15.3, gives you the most for your money. You can try it out right now for a 30-day evaluation period. Just enter the keyword **Computers** to visit the Computers channel and download the program. Or you can do a search for it at the AOL Store (keyword: **AOL Store**). For about $70, ThumbsPlus does just about everything. It displays and prints all of your digital pictures as thumbnails. In addition, you can view pictures at their full size and convert files to just about any image format.

The program is divided into two sections: a directory tree and the thumbnail section on the right. You select a directory containing your graphic files from the directory tree. If you have a lot of graphics files, they may not display automatically as thumbnails, showing as blanks instead. Clicking on the Update All button displays images from each file in thumbnails on the screen. Doubleclicking on any thumbnail displays the picture at its normal resolution. You select one, several, or all thumbnails if you want to edit them, such as doing a file conversion. Menu commands are used to do those things, or, since ThumbsPlus uses Windows 95 interface conventions, you

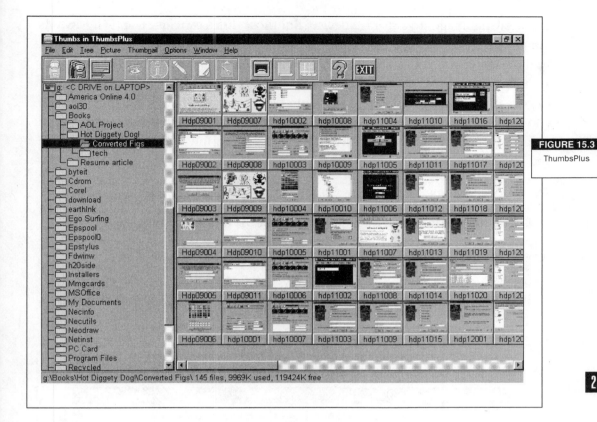

FIGURE 15.3

ThumbsPlus

can right-click on any thumbnail or group of selected thumbnails and find the actions you need right there on the shortcut menu.

The Picture Gallery

Remember the Picture Gallery? If you only have a few disks full of images or a very good memory, you might not need a thumbnails program like ThumbsPlus. The Picture Gallery (keyword: **Gallery**), as shown in figure 15.4, also displays thumbnails so you can quickly view all of the pictures on a disk, folder, or storage cartridge. However, it won't let you print, catalog, or convert your images to other file formats.

Setting Up a Digital Pictures Storage System

You've put all of this time into your digital pictures and plan to enjoy them for years to come. This means keeping them somewhere safe and accessible. You already know about saving images to a storage device. But those disks, cartridges, and CD-ROMs can pile up pretty quickly. Then, one day someone asks for those pictures of Maria's birthday party and you can't find them anywhere. Your pictures might as well be in a stack of shoe boxes. No matter what software and hardware you use, it's important to get a digital pictures storage system into place *before* you have more pictures than you can keep track of. Setting up a well-organized storage system doesn't require spending money or going to secretarial school. You simply need to put a little time and thought into it.

To set up a good digital storage system:

- **Create categories.** Think for a moment about the things you take pictures of. Most of our pictures fit into categories. You don't have to be like the Library of Congress. But you can organize your photographs by time periods (such as "Summer 1997"), recurring events (such as "Family Reunions"), vacations, work, or groups of people.

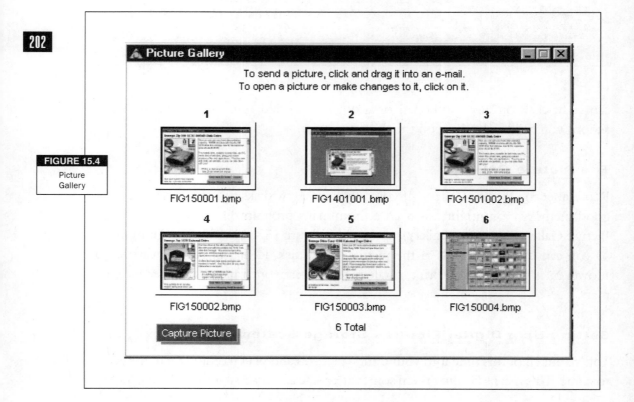

FIGURE 15.4

Picture Gallery

- **Label everything.** You should label your disks and cartridges with an easy-to-read magic marker, and also label the container you store them in. Then you never have to worry about accidentally putting a disk or cartridge in the wrong place. There's one exception to this rule—sticking something onto a CD-ROM is not a good idea. However, you should still label the CD-ROM case.

- **Print out a list.** Thumbnail programs let you easily print out your images and their filenames. But, even if you don't have one of these programs, you can still type each filename and a brief description so you don't forget what exactly you put on your disk, cartridge, or CD-ROM. You should always keep the printout with your pictures.

- **Locate storage space.** You also need a safe, accessible place to keep your digital pictures with the printouts. If your basement gets damp or your garage undergoes extreme changes in temperature, don't keep your pictures there. Zip disks and CD-ROMs fit nicely in ordinary, inexpensive CD racks, and you can slip your printouts into the cases with them. Many people also stash their disks or cartridges in envelopes and put them in a special drawer.

203

Make archiving part of your routine: Schedule a little time here and there for cleaning up your hard drive and storing your digital pictures. This keeps your computer happy and healthy, and you sane and organized. It doesn't take much time. For most people, once a month does the trick.

Most of all, set up a system you can live with. If you hate having to get a chair to reach the top shelf, don't store your pictures on the top shelf. Otherwise, you'll get annoyed every time you need to look for a picture or store a new disk, CD-ROM, or cartridge. Remember, digital pictures are supposed to be *fun,* not a dreary chore. With minimum effort you can build an impressive collection and keep adding to it. In a few years you'll be creating a photo album for Mom and Dad's golden anniversary, or surprising your children with a collection of family memories when they go away to college or move to their first apartment. You'll be the person who has the right digital picture for every occasion.

And now, congratulations to you. You are officially a digital pictures insider. So make the most of the marriage of your insider knowledge and your unique creative style to communicate and keep in touch with all the methods you've learned in this book. Send e-mail messages with pictures, audio, and special fonts. Build a Web page with digital pictures and multimedia. Send a funny photo collage to a friend who's down in the dumps. Design a killer presentation for the next department meeting. And don't forget to e-mail a digital picture to your mom. Your personal and professional life will never be the same.

Glossary

access number. A phone number used to connect to an online service.

analog. Describes the representation of information in a format that shows different levels of value or intensity. A clock with hour, minute, and second hands is an example of analog technology. (See also DIGITAL.)

antivirus software. Applications that scan computer systems and purge them of viruses. Examples: McAfee VirusScan, and Norton Antivirus Utility. (See also VIRUS.)

AOL NetFind. The search engine that's part of the AOL service.

application software. Computer programs that perform specific tasks. Word processing and database programs are examples of application software.

ASCII (American Standard Code for Information Interchange). A character set designed to be readable by most computers. An ASCII file has no formatting such as boldface or italics.

attachment. A file that is added on or attached to an e-mail file.

AU file. Audio file.

AVI. The standard video format for Windows. AVI movies can be played back with the Media Player application that comes with Windows 95.

bandwidth. The amount of information that is able to flow through a channel, expressed in bits per second (bps) or cycles per second (hertz).

bit. The smallest unit of computer information; eight bits equal one byte.

bit map. A grid that represents the bits that dictate how a picture is displayed on a computer screen. A black-and-white picture, for example, is made up of bits that are either on (expressed in code as 1) or off (expressed in code as 0). The computer processes the information provided by a bit map into pixels that make up the picture.

BMP (bit-mapped). A filename extension that indicates a bit-mapped picture.

boot. To start a computer.

bps (bits per second). A measurement of the speed of data transmission. The higher the bps rate, the faster the speed. For example, a modem that operates at 57,600 bps is considered fast, while a 14,400 bps modem is considered slow. (See also KBPS.)

browser. An application that provides access to sites on the *Internet*.

205

bulletin board system (BBS). Online sources of interactive information such as games, messages, public domain software, and shareware, usually devoted to a specific subject matter or interest group.

byte. A unit that measures hard disk storage space. One alphabet character takes up one byte of space (or 8 bits).

CD-R. Stands for CD-Recordable, a storage disk that can be written onto only once. (See also CD-RW.)

CD-ROM (compact disc read-only memory). A portable storage device used primarily for software libraries, large reference works, and multimedia applications.

CD-RW. Stands for CD-Rewritable, a storage disk that allows multiple reads and writes to the same disk. (See also CD-R.)

Channels. Major areas on the AOL service. The numerous Channels can be found on a Channels table of contents screen.

chat room. A feature of an online forum that allows two or more participants to exchange ideas and opinions in real time.

clip art. A collection of illustrations designed to be sold and used for graphic presentations.

clipboard. An area on a computer used to store cut-and-pasted material temporarily until it can be entered into a word processing application.

compress. To make files more compact so that they can be transmitted more quickly.

contrast. The relationship between light and dark areas in an image, usually referred to in terms of high contrast or low contrast.

crop. To eliminate an unwanted portion of an image.

cursor. A flashing line or rectangle on a computer screen that indicates a point of data entry, or a pointing finger that indicates a clickable link.

cyberspace. The online world.

database. A large file of information that can be accessed and searched.

desktop publishing. The use of a personal computer to set type and use graphics to produce printed materials.

digital. Describing the conversion of information into simple electronic impulses using binary numbers (1 and 0). Examples of digital technology are computers and compact discs. (See also ANALOG.)

digital camera. A camera in which images are stored digitally and downloaded to a computer without the use of film.

document. A file of text information created by a computer user.

download. To transfer information from one computer to another.

dpi. Dots per inch, which is usually a measurement of printer or screen resolution.

driver. A piece of hardware used to operate a peripheral.

e-mail. Electronic mail. The system by which individuals can communicate via computer and modem.

expansion slot. A device that accommodates plug-in cards such as *modems, video adapters,* and *sound cards.*

file compression. A process that makes files more compact, to reduce downloading time and save hard disk space. (See also COMPRESS.)

file decompression. A process that expands files that have been compressed. File decompression is necessary in order to read the files. (See also COMPRESS.)

file format. The format in which particular information is saved. Common formats for digital pictures are *GIF, JPEG,* and *BMP.*

floppy disk. A relatively small, portable, storage medium for computer data.

font. A typeface in which the alphabet and numbers are represented in a particular style and uniform size.

forum. A discussion group devoted to a particular topic, that has an online *message board* on which participants can post questions and answers; a file library containing topic-relevant applications and downloadable text files; and a conference or *chatroom* area for *real-time* dialog, interviews, and guest appearances.

frame grabber. A video camera that can capture a single frame as a separate graphics file.

freeware. Copyrighted software that can be downloaded free of charge but cannot be modified or sold. (See also PUBLIC DOMAIN SOFTWARE, SHAREWARE.)

FTP (File Transfer Protocol). The *Internet* function that enables a computer user to gain access to the *hard disk* of another computer to send and receive files.

GIF (Graphics Interchange Format). A *file format* that compresses graphic images for use online. It is used mostly for less sophisticated artwork like cartoons and line drawings, rather than photographs, which display better in the *JPEG* format.

gigabyte (GB). A measurement of *hard disk* storage space that is equal to 1 billion bytes.

grayscale. A black-and-white representation of an image.

hard disk. The main file storage area of a computer.

hardware. The physical components of a computer such as circuit boards, keyboards, monitors, and so on. (See also SOFTWARE.)

hits. Responses.

home page. The primary screen of a *Web site*; a home page serves as the entrance to a series of related screens.

HTML (hypertext markup language). The programming codes that create *World Wide Web* documents and facilitate the insertion of *links* which take users to other *Web sites*.

http (hypertext transfer protocol). The system used to transmit information from the *Internet* to a personal computer. Typically used as the first four letters of a *Web site* address.

icon. A picture on a computer screen that represents an application or a function. By clicking on an icon with a mouse, the user opens the application or file or starts a process.

image editing window. A portion of the screen displaying an image at actual size and including tools for retouching. (See also WINDOW ENVIRONMENT.)

interactive. Describes the ability to communicate online because entry of information into a computer yields a response.

Internet. A worldwide system of interconnected computers. (See also WORLD WIDE WEB.)

ISP (Internet service provider). A company that supplies a user with a connection to the *Internet*.

Jaz drive. A removable *Zip* drive, useful for storage.

JPEG (Joint Photographic Experts Group) format. A relatively high quality method of displaying pictures on a computer. JPEG is used for photographs, artwork, and paintings, for example, rather than cartoons or line drawings, which display better using *GIF* (Graphics Interchange Format).

Kbps. Kilobytes per second. (See BPS.)

keyword. A term that serves as a shortcut to get to sites on the AOL service.

kilobyte (KB). A measurement of *hard disk* storage space equal to 1,000 bytes.

lasso tool. A *masking* tool which allows selection of an area in an image by drawing freehand around it.

LCD. Liquid crystal display.

link. A connection between two documents that enables a user to access the second document from the first and vice versa.

209

masking. Selecting an area within an image to work with, using a masking tool.

megabyte (MB). A term that describes the amount of storage space on a *hard drive*. One megabyte is the equivalent of about 1 million *bytes* or about 500 pages of text.

message board. A means of online communication that allows users to post information and respond to other messages.

MIDI (Musical Instrument Digital Interface). Software application that translates data from music synthesizers for presentation on a computer.

modem. A device that allows a computer to use telephone lines to exchange information with another computer, via the *Internet*, *e-mail*, or faxes.

mouse. A device attached to a computer that is used to move the *cursor* and images around the screen.

operating system (OS). The software that is responsible for the basic operations of a computer.

PC (personal computer). A computer that serves a single user, and uses its own microprocessor to process data. Most often used to represent IBM-compatible computers as opposed to Macintosh.

PDF. Portable Document Format file.

peripheral. A piece of *hardware* connected to a computer. Examples of peripherals are printers, *modems,* and external disk drives.

pixels. The tiny dots that compose every image on the computer screen. The smallest unit of measurement on the computer screen.

"plug and play." A feature of Windows 95 and later operating systems allowing easy installation of *peripherals.*

plug-in. Any software created to extend another application's capabilities.

post. To enter a message on a *forum,* bulletin board system, or *message board*.

public domain (PD) software. Software that is not copyrighted and can be used without paying a fee or receiving permission. (See also FREEWARE, SHAREWARE.)

QuickTime. A Macintosh feature that supports the display of animated or video applications with sound.

RAM (random access memory). A computer's memory (expressed in *megabytes*) used temporarily to run applications and to display documents. (See also ROM.)

real time. A practically indiscernible delay of information transfer. A telephone conversation occurs in real time.

resampling. Adjusting the resolution of or resizing an image.

RGB. Red, green, and blue, the format used by color monitors.

ROM (read-only memory). The part of a computer's memory that is used to permanently store the essential applications that make the system run. (See also RAM.)

scanner. A device that copies graphic images or text from an external source into a computer.

screen name. The label assigned to each member of an online service that serves as a means of identification. Members of the AOL service choose screen names from between three and ten numbers and/or letters. Each account can have up to five screen names.

screen resolution. A measurement of the quality of the images displayed on a monitor, expressed in *pixels*. Examples of screen resolution measurements are 640 x 480 pixels and 800 x 600 pixels. A higher number of pixels indicates a better picture quality.

scroll. To move the text or graphics in a window vertically or horizontally by using a mouse to click on and hold an arrow that appears on the screen.

search engines. Applications that find information files online that contain certain words in its text, titles, or descriptions. A search engine may search the whole *World Wide Web* or a particular site.

search term. A word or phrase that tells a *search engine* what information to look for.

serial port. The part of the computer that works with *peripheral* devices like the *modem* and the printer to send and receive messages one *byte* at a time.

server. A powerful computer that runs a network of smaller computers.

shareware. Software available for downloading that can be tried for free or for a nominal fee before buying.

software. Application, system, and utility program(s) that perform specific functions. (See also HARDWARE.)

sound board. A piece of *hardware* that enables a *PC* to reproduce digital sound and support multimedia applications. Examples of sound boards are Soundblaster Pro, Advanced Gravis UltraSound, and Pro AudioSpectrum-16.

sound card. A card inside the computer that has independent memory and runs the computer's sound system.

special interest group (SIG). A group made up of members of a network or online service who share a common interest.

stock photos. Professional photographs contained in a collection, available for sale.

streaming multimedia. A system in which files play as they're *downloading*.

SyJet drive. A removable drive, useful for storage.

tape drive. A backup system for the computer using tape instead of disks for storage.

text-only. Straight files with no fancy printer codes, no special formatting. Often referred to as *ASCII* files.

thumbnails. Onscreen miniature versions of stored images.

TIF (Tagged Image File). A name given to a file that has scanned photographic pictures.

toolbar. A set of *icons,* usually across the top of a screen, that each represent frequently used functions.

touching up. Changing the look of an image by adjusting *pixel* colors.

upload. To transfer a file to another computer electronically.

URL (uniform resource locator). A string of characters that serves as an address for a *Web site*. An example of a URL is http://www.aol.com.

utility program. A computer program that serves to improve the operation of the system. Example: *file compression* software.

vectors. Vector programs define lines, shapes, and objects mathematically instead of by *pixels.*

video adapter. A computer component that enables the monitor to display text graphics.

video card. The computer's foundation for all imaging work. High-speed video cards are found in almost every new PC.

virus. Software application that is written with the intent that it will attach itself to files as a prank or sabotage. Viruses enter a computer via downloaded software and files. Although some viruses do nothing more than eat up valuable disk space, others have been known to damage and even destroy other applications. (See also ANTIVIRUS SOFTWARE.)

VRAM (video RAM). Memory chips for video adapters.

WAV. A sound wave, usually in 8-bit format, that stores sound files.

Web site. A location on the *World Wide Web.*

window environment. A computer application that provides user-friendly features such as dropdown menus and scroll bars in frames that display documents, databases, and drawing applications.

World Wide Web (WWW). The part of the *Internet* that links documents using *http* (hypertext transfer protocol).

'zine. An online magazine

zip. Another term for *file compression*.

zoom. To expand or reduce a picture to fit within a viewing format.

FURTHER READING

Books

25 And Under: Photographers. Alice Rose George, Editor (W.W. Norton & Company, 1996).

100 Minutes to Better Photography. Julian Padowicz (Businessfilm International, 1994).

Action Photography: Approaches and Techniques for Recording the Decisive Moment (Pro-Photo Series). Jonathan Hilton (Amphoto, 1997).

Adobe Photoshop 4.0: Tips & Tricks (Windows 95). (Ziff-Davis Education, 1997).

An Introduction to Electronic Imaging for Photographers. Adrian Davies and Phil Fennessy (Focal Press, 1994).

Authorware: An Introduction to Multimedia for Use with Authorware 3 and Higher. Simon Richard Hooper (Prentice Hall, 1997).

Capturing the Night With Your Camera: How to Take Great Photographs After Dark. John Carucci (Amphoto, 1995).

Copying and Duplicating: Photographic and Digital Imaging Techniques. Thomas A. Benson, George T. Eaton, Joseph Meehan, and Dave Howard (Silver Pixel Press, 1996).

Digital Graphic Design. Ken Pender (Focal Press, 1996).

Digital Imaging and the World Wide Web. W. David Schwaderer (Wordware Publishing, 1998).

Digital Imaging for Visual Artists. Daniel Grotta and Sally Wiener Grotta (McGraw-Hill, 1994).

Digital Photography. David D. Busch (Henry Holt & Company, 1995).

Don't Take My Picture: How to Take Fantastic Photos of Family & Friends - And Have Fun. Craig Alesse (Amherst Media, 1998).

Introduction to Imaging: Issues in Constructing an Image Database. Howard Besser, Jennifer Trant, and Howard Besser (Getty Trust Publications, 1996).

Make Your Scanner a Great Design & Production Tool. Michael Sullivan (North Light Books, 1998).

Photo/Imaging: How to Communicate With Camera and Computer. David H. Curl (Oak Woods Media, 1997).

Sell & Re-Sell Your Photos: How to Sell Your Pictures to a World of Markets a Mailbox Away (4th Ed). Rohn Engh (Writers Digest Books, 1997).

Start with a Scan. Janet Ashford and John Odam (Peachpit Press, 1996).

Stock Photo Smart: How to Choose and Use Digital Stock Photography (The Smartdesign Series). Joe Farace (Rockport Publishing, 1998).

The Creative Monochrome Image: How to Excel at Black & White Photography. David Chamberlain (Sterling Publications, 1997).

Digital Imaging A-Z. Adrian Davies (Focal Press, 1998).

The Digital Imaging Dictionary. Joe Farace (Allworth Press, 1996).

The Illustrated Digital Imaging Dictionary. Sally Wiener Grotta and Daniel Grotta (Computing McGraw-Hill, 1997).

Visual Explanations: Images and Quantities, Evidence and Narrative. Edward R. Tufte (Graphics Press, 1997).

Web Designer's Guide to Graphics: PNG, GIF & JPEG. Timothy Webster, Paul Atzberger, and Andrew Zolli (Hayden Books, 1997).

Magazines and Newspapers

Communication Arts
P.O. Box 10300
Palo Alto, CA 94303
(415) 326-6040 x26

fax: (415) 326-1648
e-mail: mikek@commarts.com

Computer Life
1 Park Avenue
New York, NY 10006
(212) 503-3500

Computer Shopper
1 Park Avenue
New York, NY 10006
(212) 503-3500

Electronic Buyers News
610 Academy Drive
Northbrook, IL 60065
(847) 291-5215
fax: (847) 291-4816

Electronic Engineering Times
610 Academy Drive
Northbrook, IL 60065
(847) 291-5215
fax: (847) 291-4816

Home PC
P.O. Box 420235
11 Commerce Blvd.
Palm Coast, FL 32142
(800) 829-9150

IEEE Multimedia
10662 Los Vaqueros Circle
P.O. Box 3014
Los Alamitos, CA 90720
(714) 821-8380; (800) 272-6657
fax: (714) 821-4010

InformationWeek
P.O. Box 1093
Skokie, IL 60076
(847) 647-6834

InternetWeek
P.O. Box 1094
Skokie, IL 60076
(847) 647-6834

MacUser
1 Park Avenue
New York, NY 10006
(212) 503-3500

MacWEEK
1 Park Avenue
New York, NY 10006
(212) 503-3500

Network Computing
P.O. Box 1095
Skokie, IL 60076
(847) 647-6834

PC Computing
1 Park Avenue
New York, NY 10006
(212) 503-3500

PC Graphics & Video
7500 Old Oak Blvd.
Cleveland, OH 44130
(440) 356-8969
Web site: http://www.pcgv.com/

PC Magazine
1 Park Avenue
New York, NY 10006
(212) 503-3500

PEI (Photo Electronic Imaging)
57 Forsyth St. NW, Suite 1600
Atlanta, GA 30303
(800) 786-6277 ext. 257
fax: (404) 614-6405

Photo District News
1515 Broadway
New York, NY 10036
(212) 536-5222
fax: (212) 536-5224

Windows
P.O. Box 420235
11 Commerce Blvd.
Palm Coast, FL 32142
(800) 829-9150

Online

A Buyer's Guide to Desktop Scanners
http://www.scanshop.com/AOL Computing Channel Live Events
keyword: **Computing Live**

AOL Multimedia Showcase
keyword: **Multimedia Showcase**
http://multimedia.aol.com/internal/index.htm

Authorware: An Introduction to Multimedia Design
http://www.prenhall.com/divisions/ESM/app/hooper/

Business Week Online's Computing Room
keyword: **Computing Newsstand**

CMPNet
http://www.cmpnet.com/

CNET.com
http://www.cnet.com/

Communication Arts
http://www.commarts.com/index.html

Computer Reseller News
http://www.crn.com

Computer Shopper
http://www5.zdnet.com/cshopper

DPI (Digital Photography & Imaging) Online Magazine
http://www.digitalphoto.com.nf/

HomePC Online
keyword: **Computing Newsstand**
http://techweb.cmp.com/hpc/

Image Scanning Resource Center on the AOL service
keyword: **Scanning**

The Larry Magid Show
keyword: **Computing Newsstand**

MacWEEK Online
http://www8.zdnet.com/macweek/

Macworld Online
http://www.macworld.com/

PC Computing Online
http://www.zdnet.com/pccomp/

PC Magazine Online
http://www.zdnet.com/pcmag

PC World Online
http://www.pcworld.com/

PEI (Photo Electronic Imaging) Online
http://www.peimag.com/

Photo District News Online
http://www.pdn-pix.com/

Sullivan's Online Scanning Resources

http://www.hsdesign.com/scanning/

Usenet Newsgroups
   alt.graphics
   comp.graphics
   comp.periphs
   comp.periphs.scsi
   comp.publish.prepress
   comp.sys.ibm.pc.graphics
   comp.sys.ibm.pc.hardware.misc
   comp.sys.mac.graphics
   comp.sys.mac.hardware.misc
   rec.photo.digital
   rec.photo.misc

Windows Magazine Online
http://www.winmag.com/

Windows Sources
http://www4.zdnet.com/wsources/

ZDNet
http://www3.zdnet.com/

221

AOL's Upcoming You've Got Pictures! Service

Q. How does it work? When dropping off a roll of film for processing at one of the more than 30,000 retail locations expected to participate in this service nationwide, you will check the "You've Got Pictures!" box on the processing form and write in your AOL screen name.— AOL will add a new "You Have Pictures!" icon to the AOL Welcome Screen, and a new voice, to let you know when your pictures have arrived.

Q. When will the service be available to members? We hope to have the service available to members by late 1998.

Q. How easy will it be to find a retailer that offers this service? Very easy. We anticipate that over 30,000 retail locations across the country where Kodak film is processed and where you see the Kodak PhotoNet online service logo will offer AOL members the "You've Got Pictures!" option. Participating retailers will display the Kodak PhotoNet online service logo.

Q. How much will "You've Got Pictures!" cost? Participating retailers will charge an additional fee to cover scanning and uploading your photos. However, there are no extra fees for the basic AOL "You've Got Pictures!" service. AOL members will have a "You've Got Pictures!" box just as they have an e-mail box. Members should check with their local retailer once the service becomes available for pricing.

Q. What is included in the additional fee? Your pictures will be scanned and delivered directly to your "AOL You've Got Pictures!" mailbox in addition to the regular prints and negatives you would normally receive. Then, you'll be able to immediately view your pictures online and choose among such options as:

- Organizing your photos into a permanent "AOL Online Picture Album, Powered by Kodak PhotoNet online;"
- Sharing them with family and friends on AOL through e-mail, or on a Web page;
- Personalizing photos through captions, cropping or enlarging to fit your needs; or
- Making them part of a moving-image [Picture Book] using AOL's Slideshow technology.

Also, for an additional fee, you will be able to order reprints and merchandise personalized with your photos, like mugs, tee-shirts, mousepads and other items through AOL.

Q. Will I need to download another version of AOL in order to get this service? No. Your AOL software will be automatically upgraded. It will be loaded the same way AOL's New Channel Line-up and other new features have been added to the service.

Q. Will just 4.0 users be able to use "You've Got Pictures!"? What about Mac users? The service will be available to all AOL members using versions 3.0 (32-bit only) or 4.0 for the Power Mac or PC.

Q. Will there be a Parental Controls feature to limit younger members' access to photos? How will it work? Yes. "You've Got Pictures!" is designed in keeping with AOL's commitment to online safety. Parents will be able to control their children's access to incoming photos, ensuring that "You've Got Pictures is a safe and family-friendly service, using AOL's Parental Controls. Accounts designated Kids or Young Teens will automatically have this Parental Control set to "off." Parents will be able to activate the "You've Got

222

Keyword Index

223

Index

ACSII, 27

ActiveX, 96, 97

address books, 4, 29, 49, 54, 55
  AOL Address Book, 19, 29, 30, 32, 55–57, 73

Adobe
  Acrobat, 178, 189–191; Illustrator, 143; PageMaker, 144, 145; PhotoDeluxe, 130; PhotoShop, 126, 142, 149, 155; Web site, 190

advanced imaging, 5

advertising, 115, 117, 118

American Greetings, 75

analog pictures, 150, 151

angle of view, 44

animation, 4, 137, 182
  AOL Press, 191; GIF, 14, 80, 94, 95, 98, 157, 179, 181, 182, 191; Flash, 184, 191; greeting cards, 75; multimedia, 184; PC Animation & Video Forum, 75, 178; postcards, 28; presentations, 138, 147; Shockwave, 76; software, 95, 184; streaming, 184; Web pages, 80, 83, 93, 98, 177, 183

announcements, 4, 35, 69, 70
  baby, 72; milestones, 73; multimedia, 75; wedding, 72

anti-aliasing, 155

AOL
  Address Book, 19, 29, 30, 32, 55–57, 73; American Greetings, 75; Ask-A-Teacher, 106; Blackberry Creek, 100, 105; channels, 10, 17, 50, 67, 75–77, 86, 93, 101, 111, 130, 138, 143, 145, 147, 178–180, 182, 202; ClickArt, 31; compressing files, 115; Desktop cinema, 98; desktop publishing, 97; Digi-

tal City, 63, 76; Digital Shop, 13, 76; Download Software, 95; Entertainment Asylum, 93; Family Album, 31; Family Computing Center, 75; Family Gallery, 62, 63; Favorites, 82, 89; file server, 82; Gallery, 50; GraphicSuite, 43; Hobby Central, 47; Instant Messages, 19, 34, 64; kids, 67, 101; Love@AOL, 62, 63; Member Services, 27; MIDI files, 186; Modem Shop, 27, 178; multimedia, 76, 93, 96, 97; music clips, 93; My Place, 92; NetFind, 33, 117; On the Net, 82, 98; Parental Controls, 101–103; PC Animation & Video Forum, 75; Personal Publisher, 4, 66, 72, 78, 80–93, 95, 97; Personal Web space, 81; Picture Gallery, 3, 10, 15, 17, 19, 20, 22, 29, 34, 35, 38, 39, 41, 43, 53–55, 58, 65, 86, 105, 107, 122, 139–141, 157, 201, 203; Picture Libraries, 30; Portrait Gallery, 2, 31, 62, 179; posting pictures on, 60; Press, 86, 181, 191; Prime Host Service, 32; Rogue Gallery, 31; Romance Connection, 63; server, 90, 91; shareware, 94, 188; Software Center, 64, 74, 78, 115; Software Shop, 53; sound files, 179; The Sound Room, 98; Store, 4, 12, 27, 53, 78, 81, 95, 110, 115, 123, 126, 130, 131, 134, 135, 172, 193, 194, 196, 202; Terms of Service, 34, 67; version 4.0, 5, 15, 19, 64, 103, 115, 184; Web browser, 73, 178, 184, 186, 189; Web Page Clip Art Creation Center, 98

aperture, 65

229

230

233

234

watercolor collections, 11

WAV, 74, 96, 185, 187

Web Page Clip Art Creation Center, 98

Web pages, 3, 32, 90, 104, 139, 159, 162, 190

adding pictures to, 31, 85, 86, 156; Adobe, 190; advertising, 117; animation, 80, 83, 93–95, 98, 157, 177, 179, 181, 183, 191; AOL Press, 181, 191; AOL server, 90, 91; associated files, 81; backgrounds for, 83, 98, 169, 171, 174; brochures, 189; business, 80, 117, 118, 178, 184, 189; cartoons, 94; clip art, 98, 173; color, 174, 175; copyright, 34; counters, 89, 90; creating, 16, 31, 35, 72, 79, 80, 82–84; Desktop and Web Publishing forum, 98; Desktop Cinema, 98; downloading, 34, 173, 175, 178,179, 181, 184; editing, 91, 92; family album, 80; file size, 175; FTP, 92; games, 179; genealogy, 54; GIF, 14, 80, 94, 95, 98, 157, 173, 174, 179, 181, 191; Home Page Improvement, 178; HotDog Pro, 185; hypertext markup language (HTML), 81, 82, 95, 96; hobbyist, 79, 80; image maps, 85, 86, 88; IRS (Internal Revenue Service), 190; JPEG, 95, 138, 156, 173; kids, 99, 105, 106; links, 81–92, 94, 95, 116, 117, 181, 189, 190; live broadcasts, 183; logos, 85, 89; Microsoft, 189; MIDI, 178, 186; movies, 83, 93, 96, 98, 178, 189; multimedia, 78, 82, 83, 93–95, 178, 181, 183–185, 189, 191, 206; music, 93; Mystic Color Labs, 122; navigation buttons, 33, 172, 173; NetFind, 33; online newsletters, 80; online parties, 66; Personal Publisher, 4, 66, 72, 78, 80–92, 95, 97, 181; photographs, 85; Prime Host Service, 32; publishing, 90, 91; RealPlayer, 97, 191; resolution, 151, 173; scrolling marquis, 80; search engines, 33, 117; Shockwave, 97, 178, 179, 184, 191; sound, 78, 80, 83, 93, 95, 98, 183, 184, 191; special effects, 172, 173; special interest, 80; text, 83–85, 88, 173; travel, 80; updating, 83; uploading pictures to, 66, 116; uploading to, 181; URL (uniform resource locator), 81, 83, 89, 95; video, 78, 80, 83, 93, 95, 96, 98, 183, 184, 189; Web Page Clip Art Creation Center, 98; Weinman, Lynda, 178;

weddings, 12, 72

Weinman, Lynda, 178

Windows, 5, 17, 123, 128, 133, 134

AVI, 96; NotePad, 95; Paint program, 14, 70, 140, 156; Sound Recorder, 187; system requirements, 18; tape drives, 200; WAV, 74, 96

WinZip, 27, 64, 65, 74, 115

WMF, 1

word processor applications, 15, 70, 78, 106, 107, 112, 114, 124, 125, 144

brochures, 137; multimedia features of, 78; newsletters, 137

Xante, 131

Zip drives, 133, 193–198, 202, 205

zoom lenses, 164

zooming, 24, 154–156, 158

Introducing the
1998 AOL PLANNER COLLECTION

The AOL Mouse Netbook

An innovative solution created exclusively for our members, this AOL MouseNetbook was designed to record and reference e-mail and web addresses quickly and easily. These convenient features include a comprehensive "glossary" of internet and technical terms and over 1,000 of AOL's most popular keywords. Customize your AOL MouseNetbook by inserting your favorite photos framed under the cover. The mousepad cover, made from Easy Track material, provides smooth movement and ease of control.

Item # 2817 $29.95

Watermen Pen for AOL Members

Designed and manufactured in Paris, this elegant black lacquer ball pen comes in the Waterman signature blue box with white satin lining.

Item # 2807 $29.95

AOL Pocket Netbook

As the internet grows and becomes a larger part of your everyday life, so does the need for a quick and easy reference guide. This uniquely designed Netbook can be helpful for jotting down your favorite places online and recording names and addresses.

Item # 2809 $15.95

TO ORDER CALL: 1-800-844-3372 EXT. 1024

The Official *AOL BOOK COLLECTION*

America Online Official Guide to the Internet, 2nd Edition

The only guide to the Internet officially authorized by America Online. This new and updated 2nd edition has all the details on AOL's latest software-version 4.0 — written by David Peal, the former Editorial Manager of America Online's Internet Connection, this book explains how to use AOL's special navigational tools to find information fast and efficiently. It also explains how AOL makes accessing and using the Internet easy. Discover the Internet's possibilities as you learn how to plan a vacation, job hunt, make friends online and even create and post your own web site!

Item # 5532 $24.95

"David Peal draws on his years of working with AOL to share insider tips that can turn your Internet experience into something truly extraordinary"
— Steve Case, Chairman and CEO of America Online.

World Wide Web Yellow Pages AOL Members Edition

This all-in-one guide to the World Wide Web, organized in familiar yellow pages format, helps you find the web sites you're looking for FAST. It contains detailed descriptions of over 10,000 sites, covering hundreds of subjects. A special introductory section, written exclusively for AOL members, explains how to navigate the WWW and the Internet quickly and expertly! The BONUS searchable CD-ROM is an electronic version of the book that lets you click on sites and travel the web hassle free!

Item # 5517 $34.99

The America Online Insider's Guide to Finding Information Online

AOL experts share the ins and outs of finding information online by explaining how to approach a search. From locating business and personal contacts, to tracking down facts, to accessing rare texts, this book helps you develop your own powers of discovery. Learn to use AOL's powerful search tools — like AOL NetFind, Find, Channel search options, and Keywords — to find the information you want—at the click of a mouse. Plus tips and ideas for searching the 50 most popular topics online. The trick is knowing where you want to go - this book will show you how to get there! From AOL Press.

Item # 5469 $24.95

TO ORDER CALL: 1-800-844-3372 EXT. 1024

The Official AOL BOOK COLLECTION

America Online Tour Guide, Version 4.0

The definitive guide for AOL members since its first edition in 1992. This all-new edition covers all the exciting, new, timesaving, fun features of AOL's latest release, AOL 4.0! Your personal tourguide to AOL, it takes you through the basics, then helps you advance, by explaining some of more powerful features that are built into the service. The original AOL guide, author Tom Lichty has helped more than 1 million AOL members get started. You'll appreciate his engaging and humorous style. Over 600 pages - everything you need to know to enhance your online experience with AOL. For both Windows and Macintosh users.

Item # 5053 $24.95

The Official America Online Yellow Pages

Want to find a particular area on AOL but don't have much time to search? Then let the all new Official America Online Yellow Pages help you find what you are looking for instantly! This complete guide covers thousands of AOL sites, providing full descriptions and keywords. It makes accessing news, stock quotes, sports stats, and even the latest entertainment scoop, as easy as typing in one word. Organized in Yellow Pages style, it will save you time & money by helping you find what you want on AOL fast!

Item # 5468 $24.95

The Insider's Guide to America Online

AOL's own Meg has written the first true Insider's guide to America Online. Experienced AOLers know Meg as the author of all the cool Inside tips at Keyword: Insider. In this book, Meg has compiled and organized those great tips to give you the inside scoop on AOL: the BEST areas and the most USEFUL tools. Learn how to manage your personal finances and investments online, find bargains on everything from flowers to automobiles, locate the best areas for kids and families, find the lowest airfares and best travel deals...and much more.

Item # 5461 $24.95

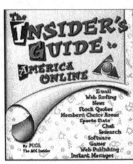

Upgrade & Repair Your PC
on a Shoestring - AOL Members Edition

Suffering from new computer envy? Well don't throw that old computer away just yet! This book provides the solid advice and information you need to make your computer run faster and do the things you want without a Ph.D. in Computer Technology and a boatload of money! Four sections talk you through upgrading your PC with lots of friendly advice and encouragement. From determining what you need, to explaining components and what they do, to the Nuts & Bolts with complete illustrations and instructions, to resources on AOL to help you through the process. This book also features the information you need to troubleshoot and make simple repairs yourself. Written in simple, easy to understand language for all computer users .

Item # 5055 $24.95

TO ORDER CALL: 1-800-844-3372 EXT. 1024

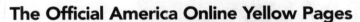

Power Up AOL AND YOUR PC

AOL Member Exclusive!

Detect and Fix modem problems!

America Online's PowerSuite

Turbo-charge your computer and make it work harder and run smarter! An AOL exclusive, the new PowerSuite CD-ROM is the only software that gives you 14 power-packed programs, utilities and games to make the most of your computing and AOL experience!

✔ Search the Web faster and easier than ever before!

✔ Add full motion video and audio to your e-mail!

✔ Update your software with Oil Change!

✔ Uninstall files easily and create archives!

✔ Easily organize and manage business and personal contacts!

✔ Deluxe Casino Games Pak! BONUS

Item # 6550 $29.95

TO ORDER CALL: 1-800-844-3372 EXT. 1024

Energize your AOL & INTERNET EXPERIENCE

An AOL Exclusive!

NEW!

AOL's Internet Accelerator Suite

Tools to make AOL & the Internet easier and more useful for you!

Start getting more from AOL and the Internet today!

AOL's Internet AcceleratorSuite

Improve your computer's performance and speed up your Web access with AOL's exclusive Internet AcceleratorSuite! Contains over 12 top-selling titles on one CD-ROM to optimize your Internet experience! Create exciting Web sites, protect your computer from viruses and keep your kids safe on the Internet!

✔ Launch to a Web site with a single keystroke!

✔ Create a Web page in as little as 15 minutes!

✔ Detect and eliminate connection problems!

✔ Add animation, sound and clip art to your Web site!

Item # 6748 - $39.95

TO ORDER CALL: 1-800-844-3372 EXT. 1024

Order your **Books and AOL Planner Collections Today**

To order by phone: **1-800-884-3372**, ext. 1024
To order by fax: 1-800-827-4595

Item #	Title	Quantity	Unit Price	Total Price
5532	AOL Official Guide the Internet, 2nd Edition		$24.95	
5517	World Wide Web Yellow Pages AOL Edition		$34.99	
5469	AOL Insider's Guide to Finding Information Online		$24.95	
5053	America Online Tour Guide, Version 4.0		$24.95	
5468	The Official America Online Yellow Pages		$24.95	
5461	The Insider's Guide to America Online		$24.95	
5055	Upgrade & Repair Your PC on a Shoestring		$24.95	
6550	America Online's PowerSuite		$29.95	
6708	America Online's GraphicSuite		$29.95	
6748	AOL's Internet AcceleratorSuite		$39.95	
2817	The AOL Mouse Netbook		$29.95	
2807	Watermen Pen for AOL Members		$29.95	
2809	AOL Pocket Netbook		$15.95	

Prices subject to change without notice.

Shipping and Handling:
Under $20.00 = $4.00
$21.00 - $30.00 = $4.25
$31.00 - 40.00 = $4.75
Over $50.00 = $5.00

Subtotal $ _____

Shipping & Handling $ _____

Sales Tax may be applicable $ _____

Total $ _____

ORDERED BY:

Name _____

Address _____

City/State/Zip Code _____

Daytime Phone Number (____) _____ - _____

SHIP TO: (if different from above)

Name _____

Address _____

City/State/Zip Code _____

Daytime Phone Number (____) _____ - _____

METHOD OF PAYMENT
☐ VISA
☐ MasterCard
☐ Discover
☐ American Express

☐☐☐☐☐☐☐☐☐☐☐☐☐☐☐☐
Account Number

Expiration Date: ☐☐ - ☐☐

_____
Signature
(Required for all credit card orders)

Send order form and payment to:
America Online, Inc.
Department 1024
P.O. Box 2530
Kearneysville, WV 25430-9935

BB24